OH, THE HUMANITY!

A Gentle Guide to Social Interaction for the
Feeble Young Introvert

JASON ROEDER

D1300003

TOW BOOKS
www.towbooks.com
Cincinnati, Ohio

11 10 09 08 07   5 4 3 2 1

Distributed in Canada by Fraser Direct, 100 Armstrong Avenue, Georgetown, ON, Canada L7G 5S4, Tel: (905) 877-4411; Distributed in the U.K. and Europe by David & Charles, Brunel House, Newton Abbot, Devon, TQ12 4PU, England, Tel: (+44) 1626 323200, Fax: (+44) 1626 323319, E-mail: postmaster@davidandcharles.co.uk; Distributed in Australia by Capricorn Link, P.O. Box 704, Windsor, NSW 2756 Australia, Tel: (02) 4577-3555

Library of Congress Cataloging-in-Publication Data

Roeder, Jason.
  Oh, the humanity! : a gentle guide to social interaction for the feeble young introvert / by Jason Roeder
      p. cm.
  ISBN-13: 978-1-58297-511-5 (pbk. : alk. paper)
  1. Success. 2. Interpersonal relations. 3. Conduct of life. 4. Introversion. I. Title.
  BJ1611.2.R573 2007
  158.202'07--dc22   2007024919

Edited by John Warner and Jane Friedman
Designed by Eric West
Illustrations by Eric West
Production coordinated by Mark Griffin

Dedication!

For the Bashful, Fearful, and Resentful

and

for My Parents

CONTENTS!

INTRODUCTION!

Your Life Has Just Changed

This may sound silly, but I want you to shake hands with yourself. Yes, I'm serious. Introductions are in order: Meet the new you! You might not realize it yet—moping, over-eating, and some sort of intricate masturbation ritual will likely remain on this evening's agenda—but you just broke the chain of indistinguishably lonely days and weeks that, to this point, you have generously characterized as your "life." By purchasing this book, you're declaring your-self ready to meet people and make friends. You're ready to have plans for the weekend, ready to be swarmed with Evites, ready to decode that baffling numerical grid on your phone, ready for strangers to call out from their porches and ask you to sit a spell, maybe cuddle. In short, you're ready to join humanity. (If, however, you're skimming this introduction and fail to actually buy the book, nothing less than Nazi-grade pariahdom awaits.)

I wasn't always your superior, of course, and, back then, I didn't have the benefit of the transformative wis-dom contained in this book, nor that of the abridged transformative wisdom available on the audio version of this book. Believe it or not, I was a particularly nervous child. Other kids were afraid of the dark; I was, too, but I was just as afraid of night-lights. I was also scared of dogs, thunderstorms, telethons, bicentennial quarters, half of all textures, and the Fonz. But what terrified me most of all was strangers, and my social anxiety only increased as I got older. No one wanted me around. I never received in-vitations to parties. My class schedule was printed without room numbers. I was all alone, sinking into despair. But one day something remarkable happened: I completely snapped out of it and wrote this book.

It's too late for you to write this book, of course, but you're just in time to live it. That's right, *live* it. While merely reading it will get you into certain speakeasies, this is not a book to be passively absorbed—it's a book to be actively obeyed. In *How to Win Friends and Influence People*, Dale Carnegie claimed that "marking and underscoring a book makes it more interesting, and far easier to review rapidly." Do no such thing on *my* pages. I have already chosen the best words, and each is as essential as the one preceding it. Concentrate on memorizing them and purchasing additional copies of them, but, most of all, concentrate on applying them.

It won't be easy. For years, your shyness has probably been misinterpreted as aloofness, arrogance, or big-time stupidity. And you've been shunned accordingly: Co-workers never ask you to lunch, and relatives forget your birthday because they've also forgotten your birth. Even cult recruiters pretend to be asleep when you pass them on the sidewalk. But it's time—right now—to put that life behind you.

It all begins with some inspirational words about this book's format.

Part one of this book, "Essential Qualities You Lack," looks at confidence, humor, curiosity, and empathy. Everyone must have these things. As you read, you might come up with other qualities that you think could be helpful in your particular situation. Put these out of your mind. All character traits beyond those discussed in part one are not to be trusted.

In part two, "Conversation for People Who'd Rather Be Home Fondling Their Record Collections, Knitting Berets for Pets They May or May Not Actually Have, or Just Sitting in a Dark Room, Dreaming of an Even Darker Room," I break down conversation into its elements. I begin with small talk. Some dismiss small talk as "idle" chit-chat, but, let's face it, you can't just walk up to someone at a black-tie event and say, "Hello. Is circumcision really necessary?" From there, I explain how to handle troublesome conversations, how to use body language ("in-person emoticons"), and how to deal with people from different and hilarious cultures.

Of course, it would be nice if some of the people you met chose to stay in touch with you, and not because you coaxed them with money, the use of your automobile, or the safe return of an immediate family member. In part three, "Making Friends That Last a Lifetime (or Until Things Just Kind of Drift)," I reveal that conversations do not always have to end with the other person faking a seizure. In fact, first encounters, if handled correctly, can lead to acquaintanceships and friendships, and the opening chapter in this section explains precisely how. Then, in the next chapter, armed with the infallible advice you've been given to this point, you will actually enter the fray. You'll learn that your new friends can be anywhere: A stranger is just a friend you haven't met and harassed yet. Like dancing? Take a tango class. Like helping people and distributing broth? Volunteer in a soup kitchen. Like drinking cocktails that for some inexplicable reason make you pass out for thirty hours before waking up on a grimy futon two states away, your only wispy memory that of a Men at Work remix? Check out the club scene. This chapter also looks at the pros and cons of using technology—from phone chat to Craigslist to Internet social networks—to help you connect with people willing to own up to the same troubling constellation of interests you have. The section's third and final chapter poses the provocative question of whether you, the reader, and I, your life-restoring exemplar, can become friends ourselves.

This introduction is just about over, but I feel obligated to inform you that the guidance contained in this book, while awesome beyond your most scrumptious erotic fantasies, does not begin to approach the totality of my knowledge. Even after you've read this book, I could very easily make you cry if I wanted to. For some reason, my editor strenuously advised against my mentioning this.

Also, if you haven't stopped shaking hands with yourself, by all means cut it out.

PART ONE!

Essential Qualities You Lack

Chapter 1

Confidence: Burying the Real You

Our dreams are messengers. Sigmund Freud, the father of psychoanalysis, is widely quoted as saying, "Hi there. Dreams are all about wish fulfillment." When I was a young man, my slumber was filled with the milking of cows, cucumbers at the ends of rainbows, and subscribing to *The Advocate*. My unconscious made its point: I was withdrawn and needed to work on my self-confidence. You have dreams, too, fantastic visions of the person you might be. Maybe you tell off your boss, or lead baboons on a raid, or order a cup of coffee without weeping. And then you wake up, feeling as microscopic as ever. Someone gave you a wedgie as you slept, and you can't formulate much of an objection. Another day of invisibility is about to begin.

Or is it? Yes, absolutely. You haven't read far enough in this book yet. While the chapters toward the end mostly reheat earlier material in the name of emphasis and word count, the information up front is as fresh and necessary as it gets. I would advise you to not leave your home for at least another fifty pages.

What Is Confidence?

The dictionary that came preinstalled in my computer defines *confidence* as "a feeling of self-assurance arising from one's appreciation of one's own abilities or qualities." In everyday life, we see confidence in the ladies' man who doesn't hesitate to ask a stranger in the supermarket for her phone number, in the actress who thrives in the Broadway spotlight, and in the lion tamer who firmly believes his training and experience will enable him to grow a new left hand. What do these people have in common? They've all come to terms with their fear. Throughout history, people have accomplished this the same way: going on television and bathing in scorpions while Joe Rogan smirks. But is there another way?

First of all, though confident people might appear as if they're acting without fear, what they're really doing is acting *despite* fear. None of them is the quivering mess you are, of course, but the paradox is that if they had no fear at all, they wouldn't need confidence to begin with. Think about your daily routine: Did you need confidence to redeem scratch-off tickets, luxuriate in pornography, or write a poem called "Most of You Will Be Sorry When I Hit the Pavement"? Of course you didn't, and that's because these tasks come easily to you. Now, this is the part where people tend to say, "That's all well and good, but what I'd like to know is whether you actually know what a paradox is." They also want practical, no-nonsense tips for boosting their self-confidence right away—without a lot of tedious psychobabble. So, without further ado, let's probe the interpersonal dynamics of your childhood.

Home Is Where the Harm Is

Your parents are to blame.

I have a confession to make: Because I could find no one else, I took my mother to prom. We weren't there fifteen minutes before she dumped me for my brother. Of course, my confidence had been undermined long before that. My father drew height notches on the kitchen wall that began at six feet and moved closer to the floor in an attempt to convince me I was shrinking. You have experiences just like these, don't you? Maybe your parents weren't overcritical but were overprotective, worried sick that their little girl would turn into an independent teenager suddenly too "cool" for the potty chair. But, in essence, the result is the same—a persistent sense of inadequacy, a stunted sense of self.

Although our parents are our earliest and perhaps most important influences, as we progress through adolescence our parents increasingly give way to the people we hang out with every day at school. I'm referring, of course, to

Obliterating Yourself With Alcohol—Responsibly

Alcohol. You can call it *booze, suds, firewater, sweet C_2H_5OH*, or *why Uncle Marvin was subdued by the other passengers*, but whatever term you use, there's no denying alcohol's power as a confidence tonic. I didn't socialize much when I was in college, and on the rare occasions when my company was sought, I usually just sat there as someone laid out the career opportunities available in the Marines or debunked the pernicious myths about Lyndon LaRouche. I didn't know anyone who could fix me up with a fake ID, and presenting a card with my thumb over the word *Blockbuster* wasn't fooling anybody.

By contrast, my only memory of turning twenty-one is sucker-punching the man who had been nice enough to resuscitate me moments earlier.

But you don't have to choose between being a dud and attacking the genitals of a paramedic. You just need to imbibe enough to help you interact more comfortably. And timing really is everything. If you're relying on booze to fortify yourself for socializing, be aware that, for many people, there's just a tiny opportunity wedged between self-consciousness and sloppiness.

8:00 P.M.–10:30 P.M. *What am I doing here? No one wants me here. I'm not funny enough. I have no anecdotes worth sharing, and there's nothing I know that everyone else doesn't already know in superior detail. P.S. Everyone can tell that I'm afraid of the whole world.*

10:31 P.M.–11:00 P.M. "Hi, my name's Carolyn. Nice to meet you. I overheard you talking about your ski trip, and I was wondering if there were any slopes you'd recommend in particular for a beginner—I mean, besides the bunny slopes!"

11:01 P.M.–??? "Look, look, I know we're a nation of immigrants. I *get* it already! Excuuuuuuuse me for being white!"

It might help if you acquainted yourself with the different types of alcohol out there, get a sense of their potency and flavor. A well-informed bartender working in a well-stocked bar can steer you toward just the right beverage. But so can I. I've sampled widely and, through a lengthy and agonizing winnowing process, have narrowed down my list to my top five.

1. Mike's Hard Lemonade
2. Mike's Hard Lime
3. Mike's Cranberry Lemonade
4. Mike's Hard Iced Tea
5. Mike's Light Hard Lemonade

At this stage, though, you shouldn't feel obligated to experiment so radically. Just find a concoction that suits you and stick with it for a while, something that doesn't make you throw up or incite you to teach people lessons they'll never forget. Of course, how much you drink is probably even more important than what you drink, and you can't always trust your judgment in this matter. Always have an impartial observer make the call.

> YOU: Oh, man, I think I'm wasted. I gotta stop. I dunno, what do you think?
>
> I.O.: Are you pussin' out on me? Cuz I gotta say—shuddup and goddamn listen for a goddamn second—I will not hereby countenance any said pussin' out.
>
> YOU: No, no, I'm cool. Just with the dizziness … And what have I done to that terrarium?
>
> I.O.: No, listen—shh!—I'm the guy telling you when you're ready to be cool.
>
> Finally, a reminder: Never drink and drive (unless, of course, the Red Bull and vodka totally cancel each other out).

guidance counselors. These important relationships can either strengthen or erode a teenager's sense of self-worth. I got lucky with Ms. Wilson. I remember having taken a personality assessment that determined I'd be best suited for work as a forest ranger or a spare part. I spent most lunchtimes in, or locked out of, her office, and one afternoon I brought her a shrub I had uprooted from the lawn in front of the school.

"Ms. Wilson, I am like this shrub," I said.

"I know, dear."

"But someday I'll grow up to be a mighty forest ranger. And then they'll all pay."

She smiled at me, kindly reminded me to take the PSAT, then quietly left the profession.

Anyway, the point to remember is that you didn't choose to have low self-confidence, and you've probably felt inadequate as long as you can remember. But you can unlearn your self-defeating programming. It isn't easy or quick, but it can be done. The next section will help you get started.

Your First Step and Some More

We've sent millions of astronauts to the moon, but the one we all remember is the first and the deadliest, Neil Armstrong. And what do we recall about him? Not his face or his name but his historic quote: "The small step of a man is what begins the journey of a thousand miles for mankind. Touchdown!" Self-confidence might seem as distant as the moon, but just by taking that first tiny step, you've advanced insubstantially closer to your goal! Are you ready? Your own mission countdown begins now.

10. *Keep a pride journal.* Before you go about changing your life, you should realize that the one you've got might not be quite as dismal as you think. I mean, yikes, I sure wouldn't want it, but when your perception of the world is distorted by long-standing feelings of inferiority, it's easy to overlook those rare, triumphant moments of mediocrity. Each night, before you go to bed, jot down a quality you like about yourself, some compliment you were paid, or some small accomplishment. If you can, shoot for one of each. For example, here's a typical entry from one of my old pride journals: "I have above-average periodontal health./

Fantasia said she'd love to show me the champagne room./ I eventually got out of the way for the ambulance." In just a month or so, you'll have a book of encouragement that you can page through whenever you're feeling low.

9. *Change your inner monologue.* Think of that voice that sabotages every effort you make to get something done, the one that whispers "You're not good enough to introduce yourself to him" or "You're way too weird and awkward to ask the bus driver for a back rub." You need to convert your interior monologue into what I like to call a "dialogue." Talk back to yourself! Remember when Al Franken's goofy *Saturday Night Live* character Stuart Smalley gazed into a mirror and said, "I'm good enough, I'm smart enough, and, doggone it, people like me"? You somehow need to do that without irony. In devising your affirmation, don't be afraid to experiment. I didn't come up with mine right away:

- ~~"When I die, no one will mourn me. They will mourn the Earth, which has to receive my body."~~
- ~~"I'm fit for nothing but whimpering."~~
- ~~"Despite my plenitude of inadequacies, it is plausible that I'll get through today without committing more than five unforgivable offenses."~~
- ~~"At least I don't have some form of gigantism."~~
- "Obey my thirst."

8. *Come to terms with failure.* You might find it hard to believe that the person who wrote this historically significant

book would have any experience with rejection. But I know what it's like to be told by a girl that she has to "wash her hair" or "baby-sit" or "shun you" on Saturday night. I've watched stranded motorists speed off on three wheels just so I wouldn't help them with their flats, and I know the embarrassment of having my credit card declined by stores and my kidney declined by desperate compatible relatives. Failure and rejection are part of life, not part of *you*. Confident people don't expect life to be one yes after another, and they learn from their mistakes. But since you see failure as an inevitable outcome and not just the consequence of some tactical or hygienic miscalculation, there's no point in learning from it. How can you get past this? The first thing you have to address is your self-consciousness. And that's number seven's specialty.

7. *Tame your self-consciousness.* We'll be covering small talk in detail, oh, I dunno, somewhere in this book. But I bring it up here because it's how we usually engage people for the first time. It's the first step in the social progression of stranger to acquaintance to friend to former friend to plaintiff. Like most socially unskilled people, you probably suffer from unbearable self-consciousness, dissociating from the most innocuous exchange.

> **ANNA:** I really like your jacket. Where'd you get it?
>
> **YOU:** *(Thinking.) I am in a social situation. I am trying to socialize right now. Now. It's almost too late to respond. But maybe if I said something now, right*

> *this second. There goes that second. I am in a so-*
> *cial situation, and now I'm thinking of blueberries*
> *for some reason. It's too late. I am in a social situa-*
> *tion. She hates me, and I am in a social situation …*

What's the best way to keep your mind grounded? Well, you can try directing your attention to your body. After all, our bodies are always in the present and don't wander off the way our thoughts do. You might concentrate on feeling the blood pulse in your fingertips, for example. If you're having difficulty with that, you can try guiding your thoughts to your body with a repeated statement such as "I am here with my nipples. I am here with my nipples …" Or you could try focusing on a detail in your surroundings—the pattern on the wallpaper, the texture of a rug, Stonehenge. Really, any little trick you can come up with to take your mind off itself will do.

6. *Look like you matter.* We give ourselves away with our appearance. Sometimes it reveals something about an occupation or an interest: The woman in scrubs wants you to know she's a surgeon, and the man crawling around in a custom-made flea collar wants you to know he's happy only if Mistress is happy. But sometimes we unconsciously let slip information that we think we're keeping to ourselves, and that includes a lack of confidence. If you're not confident, you probably think you're not worth much upkeep, and before people have even given you an opportunity to earn your self-destruction verbally, they've taken in your slouch and your scowl and your not-quite-human/not-

Five Questions With an Extraordinarily Confident Man

Thanks for speaking with me today.

No thanks needed. I'd value myself with or without your recognition.

Wow. Were you always this confident?

Of course. I've trusted myself from the very beginning. I cut my own umbilical cord.

If you could, describe what it feels like to be confident.

It's a kind of sureness of conviction, unswerving faith in your own mettle. When you're as confident as I am, your boner wakes up with *you*.

You dismissed my gratitude a moment ago. One of the characteristics of people with low self-confidence is placing excessive emphasis on the approval of others. I was wondering if you could shed some light on how you get around that.

It takes practice, but you just have to ask yourself, "Who is this person judging me?" Really, who is this person telling me I'm not cool enough or that we need to operate immediately? You've heard this before, but it really does help to imagine people in their underwear. It has a great equalizing effect, unless, of course, you're attracted to them. In that case, you'll just dwell on how out of your league they are.

> *But surely you've failed at some point in your life. How do you confront isolated failures without letting them insinuate themselves into your sense of who you are?*
>
> I try to learn from my mistakes, of course. The better I understand my mistakes, the faster I can track down the person responsible for my making them.
>
> *Fascinating. One last question: If the people cherishing this book wanted to do one thing right this second to boost their self-confidence, what should it be?*
>
> I used to suggest to people that they run out and talk to someone without thinking. The idea was that they'd blurt out a hello to a neighbor before their self-consciousness had a chance to kick in. Then I found out many of them were walking up to strangers and saying things like "Velcro" or "urethra" before going totally mute.
>
> *Well, I know you don't need to hear it, but I just wanted to say thanks again. You've really been inspirational.*
>
> I knew I would be. I've always known.

quite-raptor fingernails. Without saying a word, you've made a terrible impression. Later on, I'll show you how to put body language to work. You'll never have another Secret Service agent track your movements again.

5. *Change your environment.* You find yourself in a strange neighborhood. All the car windows are bashed in, the

storefronts are boarded up, and the gun-toting pimp rats are covered in graffiti. Without meeting any of the actual people who live in this blighted place, you would probably feel uneasy. That's because an environment reveals something about the state of mind of the people who inhabit it, whether it's a whole community or just you. Now let's say a stranger finds himself in your apartment. What would he make of you? What would he think your aspirations were? Do you have interesting books and magazines and adult-education catalogs? Pictures of family and ... others? Sporting goods? Musical instruments? A calendar with something written in the boxes besides preprinted reminders for the spring equinox and Administrative Professionals Day? Is there anything at all in your dwelling besides an air mattress, an old loaf of bread, and the wrench you use to beat it with? Like your appearance, your environment can reinforce your pre-existing feelings about yourself. When you look around your house, do you think, "The person who lives here is active and social, someone who seems to get along well with people"? Or do you think, "The person who lives here is ready to go to war with the government at any time"?

Fortunately, your surroundings can be used to alter your state of mind, not just reinforce it. So, fake the new you for a while. Open your windows, buy light bulbs, and hang something on your wall besides that framed photo of you sulking. Also, keep a copy of this book in every room (porches and closets count as rooms), and be sure to have

Amazon send you a fresh one every week. Your very sanity depends on this. (Also, refrigerators count as rooms.)

4. *Dump your friends.* All together now: "But I don't have any friends!" Yes, I know. (In the last item, as you might recall, I ribbed you about your friendlessness. If you missed it, don't worry. I'll probably undermine you again soon enough.) The truth is that you probably don't spend your whole life in total isolation. But the few companions you do have no doubt share your frustrating habits and will shame you into not associating with people outside your small dysfunctional clique. (If you've ever made the effort, you know the sting of "Oh, don't let us stop you, Ms. I'm Too Good for a Listless Farce of a Life.") Here's the truth: They're holding you back. Here's more of the truth: You're holding them back. For everyone's sake, it's best to part company.

In adhering to standard NASA launch protocol, I'm going to stop the countdown at four. You are go for liftoff—but you're no "socialnaut" yet. Sure, confidence will get you off the ground, but you'll need more than that to maintain social orbit or whatever. For one thing, you'll need a sense of humor, and the next chapter will help you develop yours. Some people make a living with theirs, while others desperately, desperately want to, you have no idea. For conversational purposes, however, all you need is an innate sense of timing you're just born with or you aren't. You'd be surprised how far a few chuckles can take you. After all, laughter's not just for behind your back.

Chapter 2

Humor:
Harnessing Your Inner Wayans Brother

We know that nothing can help us win someone over faster than being funny. We also know that nothing can crumble our self-esteem faster than when our sense of humor misfires—our jokes are flat, our anecdotes are long-winded and pointless, our topical references predate the triceratops. Not long ago, I was splitting a bottle of Chianti at one of my favorite *ristorantes*, L'Originale Alfredo di Roma in Epcot's Italy pavilion. I was there to console my businessman friend John, who that very day had addressed a ballroom full of colleagues at a convention. He had decided to start his address, which was on teamwork, with an anecdote from his domestic life:

"My wife and I have this large potted plant that we wanted to transfer from the living room to the porch, so it would get more sunlight. First, she held the screen door open while I tried moving the plant, but then we decided that moving the plant was a two-person job. So she took off one of her sneakers and propped the door open with it. We were then able to very easily complete the transfer of the plant."

At this point in his notes, John had written in parentheses, "Pause ten to thirty seconds for laughter." He just couldn't understand the curdling silence he received instead. "What's funny was that my wife had on *one* sneaker, not two," he told me. "What kind of way to walk around is that, all slightly uneven for a couple of minutes?"

Now, I personally found my friend's story sidesplitting, but that's only because I'd seen John's plant, and it's hysterical. But John had known the risk he was taking, and, discouraged as he was, we both knew he'd try again someday. The payoff is just too tantalizing to be ignored.

Are You Funny?

If your friends exist, maybe they constantly tell you that you're funny. Does that mean you actually *have* a sense of humor? Not necessarily, though it might mean your friends do. And even if their praise is sincere, you don't know if it's credible enough to matter. Maybe you're sitting around watching *Last Comic Standing,* and one of your friends says, "You know what? I think you're just as funny as those guys." You are enraged, of course, just as you would be had she said, "I just read this essay where Andy Rooney really tore state mottoes a new one. It reminded me of you." But if you can't rely on friends and family, where can you get the honest, authoritative opinion you think you deserve? Sure, you could take a comedy class, where your instructor would take his mind off his screenplay just long enough to assure you that nothing could be fresher than your observation that women sometimes flirt with police officers to get out of speeding tickets. You could also read a book, but an author, of course, doesn't actually know you—not like I do.

Be Your Own Punch Line

All of us have some sort of peculiarity. Shown above: someone with a stutter.

Before you get to mining the tragedy of others for your amusement, it's important that you learn to laugh at yourself. And I'm not referring to the brittle, resigned type of laughter you're already so horribly used to, the kind you emit when life once again follows through on its commitment to thwart your every grasp at happiness. I'm talking about not taking yourself too seriously—and letting others know you don't! Stand-up comics base a lot of their material on their flaws, of course, but the principle can be applied in almost any conversation.

In the example below, notice how Christine gently pokes fun at her skin tone.

> **KERRY:** I'd like to take my nephew to the beach. Which do you like best?
>
> **CHRISTINE:** Honestly, I'm not much of a beach gal. I'm way too pasty. I get a sunburn in a movie theater.

How do you think Kerry feels about Christine? If you're Kerry you're thinking, "Wow! Here's a woman who's easy-going and approachable. And now it's time to move on to someone who can actually answer my original question." Also, keep in mind that self-deprecation can backfire. For one thing, you have to apply it with a light touch.

> **KERRY:** Do you get out to the beach much?
>
> **CHRISTINE:** Not really. I'm way too pasty. I look like a missing person who got pulled from the river two weeks too late. Or maybe some sort of clammy, semi-amphibious monster. And have you noticed how visible my veins are? It's like I'm wearing my circulatory system.

You should also choose the content of your self-critical remarks carefully. People often joke about their weight, for example. Sometimes, disabled people will use humor to call attention to their disabilities, so the people they're interacting with won't feel self-conscious about noticing them. Still others will make light of their klutziness or their inability to draw well. But there are some imperfections that need not be revealed.

> **DAWN:** I'd like to have a garden, but I know I don't have a green thumb. I bet I couldn't keep a cactus alive for more than a week!
>
> **JAMES:** Yes, and I can't stop making obscene phone calls to the recently widowed.

Once you've learned how to appropriately call attention to your own faults, you can start taking chances with the world around you. But it's not that easy. Over the years, clients have griped to me about how their efforts at humor have earned them nothing but awkward silence, forced chuckles, and excommunication. I've collected their mistakes and present some of them here because each illustrates an important point.

> **"WHY'D MY AIDS JOKE BOMB?
> I MEAN, I WAS AT AN AIDS BENEFIT."**

Knowing Your Audience

Here's an ordinary sentence: "I just got this great barbecue grill, and I wanted to invite all of you over for some tasty ribs later on." Floating here on the page, these words might seem mouthwatering. Now insert them into the Gettysburg Address. They're not quite so delicious anymore, are they? That's because language, as we experience it in our everyday lives, does not occur in a vacuum. It happens at a place in time and in someone's ear. Humor is very much the same. If we overlook the context, disaster awaits.

First of all, look around. Get a sense not just of your physical surroundings but also of the emotional environment. Do the people at the fund-raiser seem in the mood for a giggle or more inclined toward eradicating human trafficking in our lifetime? Is the man seated next to you in the waiting room more interested in your story about the zany tour guide you had in Morocco or in whether he'll regain his senses of smell and taste? Of course, just because a situation wouldn't ordinarily call for humor doesn't mean humor is necessarily inappropriate. In fact, in skilled hands, it can heal. My brother-in-law Miles returned from a family vacation a few years ago to find the home he shared with my sister and their two daughters flattened by a mudslide. I remember the phone conversation he and I had that very day:

> **MILES:** I can't believe it. My whole life, gone. I don't know where to begin putting it back together again.
>
> **ME:** Listen, if there's anything at all you need— cash, a place to stay, a henway, whatever— just tell me.
>
> **MILES:** Thanks, Jason. Naturally, we just dropped twenty thousand dollars on a new roof!
>
> **ME:** So, no henway?
>
> **MILES:** No, we'll get by, I guess. Anyway, I'd better go.
>
> **ME:** Wait, wait. You don't even know what a henway is, do you? Why don't you ask me?

MILES:	Look, I'm really distracted. They're bulldozing, and I can hardly hear you …
ME:	Henway! Henway! You have to ask me what one is!
MILES:	What is it?
ME:	For fuck's sake, Miles! You just have to say, "What's a henway?"
MILES:	Why don't you just tell me?
ME:	If you don't say, "What's a henway?" in the next five seconds, you and my sister can forget about staying with me. You can just sit in the muck. It's too bad I won't be there to watch your kids stumble upon the carcasses of their pets.
MILES:	Fine, what's a henway?
ME:	About nine pounds!

In the midst of Miles's agony, I slipped in a subtle joke. Of course, no joke can rebuild a home, but, if applied correctly, humor can remind someone that, even in our darkest hours, if we can keep laughing, we can keep living.

Now, let's say you're at a cocktail party—wine is flowing, music is playing, no one is wearing the underwear they arrived in. You look around and say, "Yep, it's a good place for funny." But just because the setting's auspicious doesn't mean that anything goes. People, even at parties, carry with them an array of characteristics and life experiences that will affect their receptiveness to your humor. The best thing to do is give people the chance to reveal themselves. You're always taking a risk when you try to be funny, but if you hold tight for just a little bit, you'll pick up some clues.

> **TOM:** So nice to meet you. No, I don't know the host of the party personally, just through a mutual acquaintance. Be advised that I find nothing in the world more hilarious than when one friend says to another, "How's that rash?" in a crowded, confined space.

> **ROYA:** I've been in higher education for twenty years now. I just can't imagine working in an office anymore. And do you know any "yo mama" jokes pertaining to body hair?

It really is that simple.

> "DID YOU HEAR ABOUT THAT TRAIN CRASH? EVERYONE ABOARD WAS KILLED, INCLUDING A GROUP OF FOURTH-GRADERS ON THEIR WAY BACK FROM A TOUR OF A CANDY FACTORY. IT'S FUNNY BECAUSE IT'S TRUE, RIGHT?"

Honing Your Observations

Unlike prop comedy, which requires easy access to eight-foot pencils and sausage nunchucks, observational humor is always good to go. But maybe it's a little too user-friendly. Just because something occurs or exists doesn't mean it's funny.

> **PHYLLIS:** Ever notice how some food needs to be refrigerated?

There's actually a stand-up comic named Jerry Seinfeld who specializes in observational humor, and if you're ever lucky enough to catch his act somewhere, you'll see that he doesn't just recite banalities. He makes a larger point or draws absurd connections between two superficially unlike phenomena. You're no comedian, but you can still effectively use observational humor in your social interactions.

> **BARRY:** What's with the unicycle? I mean, it's like someone had a perfectly good bicycle on his plate and said, "I'm stuffed. You want half?"
>
> **GILBERT:** Actually, the unicycle is widely believed to have originated out of a quirk of the penny-farthing bicycle. It seems the tiny back wheel would rise up, leaving riders pedaling on just the oversize front wheel. Some saw this as a challenge and tried maintaining their balance as long as possible. This challenge was incorporated into the design of what we now know as the modern unicycle.
>
> **BARRY:** My point exactly.

> **"I FORGOT TO MENTION THAT THE FARMER ALSO HAD A DAUGHTER."**

Telling a Joke

Ordinarily, observational humor is easy to work into a conversation. But since you probably improvise about as well as a voicemail greeting, odds are you'll find it difficult

Fresher Than the Prince of Bel-Air: Keeping Your References Up-to-Date

The world of pop culture provides a never-ending stream of material for observational humor. (I do a pretty g-g-g-good Max Headroom impression myself.) Unfortunately, it isn't always easy to track cultural ephemera. That's why I'm providing this handy set of lists. You should photocopy it, laminate it, and keep it with you. Then, any time you need a cheat sheet for "what's hot," you can simply take a peek.

TOP FIVE MOVIES

Borat: Cultural Learnings of America for Make Benefit Glorious Nation of Kazakhstan
The Santa Clause 3: The Escape Clause
Flushed Away
Saw III
The Departed

TOP FIVE SINGLES

"My Love" (Justin Timberlake featuring T.I.)
"Smack That" (Akon featuring Eminem)
"Fergalicious" (Fergie)
"Money Maker" (Ludacris featuring Pharrell)
"Lips of an Angel" (Hinder)

TOP FIVE TV SHOWS

Desperate Housewives
Sunday Night Football
Grey's Anatomy
Dancing With the Stars
CSI

to use effectively. A joke is something else. You don't need to rely on the world around you. You can rehearse a joke and drop it into conversation any time you've had enough of some bore droning on about his job or his kids or his piranha attack. Just say, "This guy walks into a bar …," and you've got an audience. But then what?

Before you get started, be sure you actually know your joke. Have it legitimately memorized. There's nothing quite as mortifying as saying to a group of eager listeners, "Well, you get the gist of where I was going with the rabbi and whatnot." Also, don't hype your joke. If you declare your joke funny, you raise the bar for it and stoke the anticipation of the people hearing it. (Assume that we're talking about strangers or the most marginal of acquaintances. Persons more intimate with you will, of course, have realized long ago that their expectations cannot be miniscule enough.) Finally, don't ask people if they want to hear a joke—of course they do. The exception to this rule is a potentially offensive joke. In this case, discreetly make sure that you've got the right group of listeners.

> **YOU:** Is anyone here a redneck or a crocodile that's been forcibly sodomized?

So you're ready to begin. The best joke is a streamlined joke. Stick to common settings such as heaven and whorehouses. If you have to devote the first fifteen minutes of your joke to getting people up-to-date on advances in nanotechnology, you're being far too obscure. Likewise, character details are necessary only inasmuch as they set up the punch line. Look at the following example. There's a much shorter, tidier joke embedded within. Can you find it?

A man parks his 1993 Pontiac Grand Am, enters an apartment building, and takes the elevator to the eighth floor. He turns left, but then remembers he meant to turn right, so he does. He walks down to room 817. Knock! Knock! The man hears the shuffle of slippers and knows he's being studied through a peephole. Finally, in that rasp that could only belong to Chico, the man hears, "Who's there?" The man wonders why he came. Had he learned nothing? He takes a deep breath and says, "Falafel."

"Falafel who?"

And the man has to smile—as if Chico didn't know! But the man realizes he's out of options, so he says the only thing he can say: "Falafel my bike and skinned my knee!" The chain is unlatched, the door opens. The man steps into a dimly lit living room redolent of stale cigar smoke and despair.

Yes, there's a perfectly good knock-knock joke in there that just needs to be distilled from the extraneous information. If you still can't find it, try reading the text again, but this time omitting the model year of the man's Grand Am.

Finally, there's the punch line. To borrow a term from high finance, the punch line is your "money shot." Getting it right could mean the difference between an immediate awkward ending to an acquaintanceship and an eventual awkward ending to an acquaintanceship. The best thing you can do is practice your delivery, remembering not to be overeager with your punch line, and hope that you're not one of the many people who just can't tell a joke. I forgot to mention that might be a problem for you.

Putting It All Together

This paragraph actually has nothing to do with putting it all together—honestly, it just seemed like an appropriate subhead with which to end a chapter. And that's where we are, in fact. Chapter three deals with curiosity. Any interpersonal connection requires mutual curiosity—and I mean the engaged type of curiosity, not the everyday variety behind questions such as "What time is it?" and "Is there porn in this hotel room?" If you want to forge authentic friendships with people, you have to pretend like they matter.

Kaboom! So You've Bombed

"So, the guy says, 'How do you think I rang the doorbell?'" It's the punch line from a mildly amusing joke about a quadruple amputee with a telescopic cock. In someone else's hands, the joke would have done no harm and might even have earned a few laughs. But you botched it. One of your listeners looked away in disgust, while another wished she'd remembered to bring her gun to the Christmas party. A nearby housefly decided that even two weeks was too long to live. So, what now? It's been many years since I've personally been in this position, and my sense of humor is now so infectious that I can make milk shoot out of people's nostrils when I'm the one drinking it. Still, I'll admit that in my youth I had the worst sense of comedic timing. I was the only kid who told jokes about the space shuttle *before* it exploded. But, as I developed, I learned what to do when your joke goes terribly wrong.

1. Don't revive the joke. Imagine an ER doctor. Tears are running down his face and seeping into his surgical mask. He interdigitates his hands and sinks the heels of his palms into the chest of a flatlining patient. "Come on! Damn it, come on!" he says. He thinks he heard a pulse just a second ago, and the nurse with the cell-phone ringtone called "Healthy, Steady Heartbeat" is afraid to speak up. But it's soon clear that the doctor's exertions are futile and, frankly, maybe a little showoffish, as if he kinda liked the way his voice sounded calling for all those cc's of adrenaline. It's all over for the patient, but the doctor just won't admit it. In case you were wondering, this scenario has something to do with you and your joke, and now I'll reveal it: This doctor is you, and the patient is your joke. Just let it expire on the table.

2. Don't tell another joke. Let's see, you've already ruined your first, and presumably best, joke, and the ensuing silence has left you stupefied and wishing you were home in the fort you constructed entirely out of stuffed animals. Now is not the time for Plan B. You will only make things worse, reaching deeper and deeper into your repertoire, until there's nothing left to do but paraphrase a sketch you saw on *Mad TV*.

3. Don't get angry. It's easy to blame a failed joke on someone else's sorry lack of wit, intelligence, or cruelty. There's no point in making a scene, however, not when you can redeem yourself by showing a sense of humor about your flop. You can defuse the tension by saying, "If you thought *that* was funny, I've got a million more just like it!"

Then, when you get home, you can prick your finger and smear the names of everyone who didn't laugh onto your enemies list.

Chapter 3

Curiosity:
"Oh, Do Go On About the Peace Corps!"

If the people who attend my many book signings have one thing in common it's outrage over the fact that I not only charge for my signature but also charge for giving the book back. But there's something else these people share: frustration over the fact that even when they're lucky enough to enter into a conversation, it never lasts more than a few sentences before withering into awkwardness. Why? Read the following exchanges and see if you can figure it out:

JEN: I like my neighborhood. You're not tripping over bistros and boutiques, but you still feel safe walking around at all hours.

TONY: I've often been told I resemble a black, chubby Morrissey.

PATTY: I'm the last person you'd think would skydive, but there I was, looking down on some cow pastures from ten thousand feet in the air. Finally, I—

JAY:	Silence! It is I who will speak now!
PEDRO:	I really loved South Carolina, but I knew if I wanted a good high-tech job, I'd have to relocate to a big city. So, here I am.
ANNE MARIE:	Well, I'm guessing someone's already beat me to it, but let me welcome you to Boston. What sort of high-tech work are you interested in? And what do you think of Beantown so far? Had a chance to check out the Red Sox yet?

Reread these exchanges carefully, paying particular attention to the comments of Tony, Jay, and Anne Marie. Do you think any of them made a good impression? Which of them was able to keep the conversation going and "sow the oats of friendship"? Tony responded to Jen with a bizarre, self-centered non sequitur, while Jay tyrannically seized control of the conversation. But what about Anne Marie? Do you suppose *she* left a negative impression? The answer, of course, is yes, because her conversation was actually taking place in Seattle, not Boston. Nevertheless, Anne Marie had the right idea. Curiosity makes all the difference.

What Is Curiosity?

If you want the answer to this question—guess what?—you're curious! You want to know about the world around you. As a child, you were naturally inquisitive.

Remember curiosity?

When you were small, you might've shaken your Christmas presents. As you entered adolescence, maybe you puffed a cigarette, tried on the undergarments of an oppositely gendered parent, or ran a gauntlet of crowbars so the Crips would embrace you. But as you entered adulthood, your wide eyes narrowed. New information no longer seemed to matter as much, and the world out there could safely be ignored or, at most, TiVo'd and skimmed. Now it's all about you—and, occasionally, the parrot with whom you've pathologically bonded.

All of us are caught up in our own lives, yet we still seek out other people. Sometimes we have specific needs—a chess opponent, a gym partner, solo females or maybe select couples to make the orgy tolerably proportional—but, generally, most of us just want to have our thoughts and feelings validated. Now, examine your thoughts and feelings for a moment. You seriously want someone to validate *those*? Yikes. But if that's what you're after, you're going to have to return the favor, because everyone else is as self-centered as you are. You will have to be actively curious.

Quiz: Are You Curious?

As I was walking home one evening, I suddenly recalled that a new flavor of fitness water was scheduled to be released that day, but I wasn't anywhere near a convenience store. Then I remembered that there was a Russian market, an adorable establishment with a sign whose letters all looked like broken numbers, not far from my house. I passed it all the time and always wondered what they sold there. I decided it was time to give in to my curiosity. What began as a simple errand blossomed into a gustatory transcontinental adventure that ended with me verbally abusing an elderly baker for not making his *sharlotka* apple pies with Splenda. And I wouldn't have had this opportunity if I hadn't acted on my curiosity.

What about you? Are you curious? Mildly curious? Numb to new experience? Answer the questions below and find out:

1. One lazy Sunday afternoon, a man you've never met before arrives at your front door and claims to be your real father. What do you say to him?

    a. "What?! This is crazy! Are you joking? You've got some explaining to do!"

    b. "Okay, I'll be your kid—for now. I may want to ask you about this down the line."

    c. "Whatever. Just tell me what my new last name and inherited health risks are."

2. Your phone bill is much, much higher than usual. What is your reaction?

   a. "Something doesn't seem right here. I'm going to inspect my statement carefully and start asking some questions."

   b. "Well, I kinda wish I knew what a 'Spork Accessibility Fee' or a 'Hulkamania Surcharge' was, but I guess it's not my job to know, right?"

   c. "Eh, I probably called Mars."

3. It's late at night, and there's a ruckus downstairs. What do you do?

   a. Quietly get out of bed, grab a flashlight and a baseball bat, and tiptoe onto the landing to get a better look.

   b. Sit up in bed. Listen for a very obvious sign of trouble such as a pirate chantey. Call out a "Hello?" that gets lost in your yawn. Don't bother to try twice.

   c. Although it's not raining out, just pretend it's thunder that said, "Two hands with the stereo, dumb-ass! Two hands!"

4. "Hello. I'm calling with your test results."

   a. "Oh, God, this is it. I haven't slept in three weeks. Okay, doc, break the news to me."

   b. "That's really fab. Listen, could you just e-mail those when you get a chance? I'm actually on the other line with some guy who's got the wrong number."

   c. "I don't know, just give them to charity."

5. Just before bed, your spouse tells you that she has a secret to reveal, something involving herself, sex, one of your brothers, emptying your bank account, and framing you for a warehouse fire. What do you say?

a. "My God! Don't just sit there, spill it!"

b. "Whew, that sounds like a lot of info. Could you just give me, like, an executive summary or something?"

c. "Honey, Jimmy Kimmel's trying to do his monologue, okay?"

6. Aliens have landed on your street.

a. "Aliens! What do they want?"

b. "Aliens. What do they want, a medal?"

c. "Wake me when the probing begins in earnest."

7. You're waiting at the bus stop. A man in a bunny suit staggers toward you and collapses at your feet. Arrows are lodged in his back, and with his last, blood-flecked breath he presents you with a package that has your name on it. What do you do?

a. Gasp. Wait for the shock to subside, then cautiously open the package for which this man/animal has surrendered his life.

b. Shrug. Open the package once you've finished reading the newspaper's list of celebrity birthdays.

c. Yawn. Nudge the box with the tip of your shoe. If it somehow doesn't feel like anything good or whatever, toss it.

8. "Would you like to play 20 Questions?"

   a. "Love to!"
   b. "Is it a blowfish? Either way, I'm done guessing."
   c. "Hey, quizmaster, why don't you shove an animal, vegetable, and mineral up your ass?"

Your Curiosity Quotient revealed: Give yourself two points for each *a* response, one point for each *b*, and zero points for each *c*.

0–5 Fundamentalist or Rock
You're a lot like a fundamentalist or a rock.

6–10 Infophobe
All you really need to know you've avoided since kindergarten.

11–14 Gossip Monger
There is no co-worker tragedy not worth knowing or disseminating or exacerbating.

15–16 Super Sleuth
You probably spend a dozen hours a week in your neighbors' garbage.

Curiosity makes people feel important, no matter how small or destructive their contribution to society may be. It breaks down barriers. For example, back when I was CEO of a multinational corporation, I personally directed a human-resources liaison to get to know my employees on a more intimate level—family, hobbies, aspirations, and so on. That may seem like a waste of time, but it was absolutely invaluable during a period of executive-level instability, reconfiguration, and mass incarceration. I had the unfortunate duty of cutting loose hundreds of devoted and superfluous employees. When you read the excerpt below, put yourself in the place of one of the workers. How would you have felt if you had been let go *without* this personal touch, if your boss had simply sent you to the junkyard like an obsolete piece of machinery? Though I myself have proven irreplaceable throughout my own professional life, my understanding is that losing a job is never easy. But there's a right way to break the news.

To: employeegroup@roedercorp.com
From: jroeder@roedercorp.com
Subject: Sad tidings for some of you :(

It is with great reluctance that I terminate the following employees, all of whom must surrender their IDs no later than 5:00 p.m. this afternoon. (Day-care workers have been instructed to shun the children of these employees as of that hour.) An uncatered, unpaid, unlit farewell party for those departing will be held in the break room at 4:50 p.m.

Anderson, Sheryl (Best of luck with: opening a bed-and-breakfast someday.)

Becker, Gary	(Best of luck with: never paying another dime of bloodsucking alimony.)
Bradley, Derrick	(Best of luck with: feeling that you finally found a job that's really more like a family.)
Chang, Eric	(Best of luck with: making a threesome happen.)
Dietrich, Julie	(Best of luck with: daughters named Sarah and Betsy and I can't read the name of the third in my notes, but it's the really sick one.)

How was I able to accomplish this? I was curious. I had taken the time to get to know my employees, and that's why—my cringing, overcompensated advisers assured me—I never lost their respect, even under the worst of circumstances. Curiosity isn't just for business, of course. In *How to Win Friends and Influence People*, Dale Carnegie wrote, "You can make more friends in two months by becoming interested in other people than you can in two years by trying to get other people interested in you." Although I've supplanted Carnegie as the authority on these matters, he still has a point: You can't do without curiosity when you're trying to make friends. But how does curiosity actually manifest itself in conversation? It starts with listening.

Hearing vs. Listening

Hearing and listening have been waging bloody war for as long as anyone can remember. It's important you know the difference between the two, not only because it will help you in conversations, but also because you'll know which neighborhoods audiologists consider combat zones. Hearing is simply a perceptive event that just happens as long as your ears work. Listening is hearing, plus concentration and an extra syllable. It's a choice you make when you're gathering information. That's what curiosity is all about, and you suck at it. It's not just you, though. Recently, a team of socioperceptionists analyzed the average day of a number of Americans, distinguishing between audio phenomena that were attentively listened to and those that were heard with indifference. A representative excerpt follows. (Listened-to events are in bold italics.)

7:30 A.M.	Alarm rings, dog barks, coffeemaker gurgles, spouse revisits accusation of emotional cruelty from night before.
8:00 A.M.	Vibrating toothbrush hums, vibrating razor hums, vibrating contact lens hums, shreds cornea.
8:30 A.M.	Car door shuts, engine starts, radio clicks on, ***morning deejay affects effeminate lisp to ridicule underachieving ballplayer.***
1:30 P.M.	Supervisor reviews quarterly objectives, stresses interdepartmental communication; consultant conducts diversity workshop.

3:00 P.M.	Mother calls, pleads.
4:30 P.M.	**Co-worker cries about sudden bad news behind closed door.**
6:30 P.M.	**Drive-through speaker confirms order of Crispy Chicken Sandwich combo meal.**
9:00 P.M.	Spouse says, "I mean, I truly do wonder if you even have a soul."
11:00 P.M.	**Television announces tonight's winning Lotto numbers.**

Fortunately, if you're prepared to put in the hours and hours of hard work, becoming a better listener isn't all that difficult. In any conversation, your partner will offer cues that you can use to keep a conversation rolling.

> BRENDA: I would like to talk about recent books I've read.

Did you catch that? What's Brenda's "interest agenda"? What do you think she might want to discuss? Believe it or not, embedded in that sentence is all the material you need for a great follow-up. What word jumps out at you? Put another way, what's Brenda's "curiosity key"? Did you say "books"? Well, try it.

> BRENDA: I would like to talk about recent books I've read.
> YOU: Tell me of these books.

Congratulations, the ball is rolling. But let's say the topic of books worries you because the book currently in your hand is the only one you've read since a paperback twenty years ago with the words "Inspired by actual events on *Knight Rider*" on the cover. No need to panic. For one thing, you can try nudging the conversation toward interesting magazines, pamphlets, or coupons you've come across. Or, if literacy itself is what troubles you, there's always a way to gently redirect to another topic. All you have to do is *listen*.

> **BRENDA:** I would like to talk about recent books I've read.
>
> **YOU:** Tell me of these books.
>
> **BRENDA:** I finally got around to rereading *The Great Gatsby*. I read it in high school, of course, but you approach classics differently as an adult than you did as a sixteen-year-old who has to write a stupid paper.
>
> **YOU:** Well, it's so much easier to actually enjoy a book when it isn't presented as a task. And can you get herpes just by someone coughing on you?

Through active listening, you were able to steer a conversation toward more comfortable terrain, but without making Brenda feel like you were wasting her time or vice versa. Now, Brenda's "lifestyle matrix" was fairly straightforward. But it's not always so clear. In these cases, you still have to listen, but there's a little more legwork required.

> **CHARLES:** Walnuts.

If you want to talk about walnuts with Charles, you can simply say, "I adore walnuts! They add a great crunch to salad. How do you like to serve walnuts?" However, what if you have no desire to talk about walnuts but also don't consider that single word to be a very good springboard to a different topic? First, remember that curiosity isn't just about information gathering: it's also about making someone feel important. If you're going to attempt a radical transition, don't do it without first validating the other person.

> **CHARLES:** Walnuts.
>
> **YOU:** Ah, yes, walnuts.

Now that you've acknowledged Charles's contribution, you can attempt to shift the conversation. The best way to do this is not to pick a topic that might interest only you, but to remain focused on Charles. This is a good place for *visuaistening*, an easy shorthand way of remembering the phrase *visual listening*. People don't only reveal information with words, after all. Is there something about Charles that catches your *eye*?

> **CHARLES:** Walnuts.
>
> **YOU:** Ah, yes, walnuts. Say, I've noticed you're wearing three sweatshirts but no pants. I bet there's a great story behind that.

Charles may have a perfectly ordinary explanation for his attire. It doesn't matter, though. You've kept the focus on him—but spared yourself a dull exchange on walnuts!

Can I Be Too Curious?

I didn't always have the answer to this question. It took years of gasps, mountains of cease-and-desist letters, and endless stun-gun discharges for me to realize that, in fact, you can want to know too much too soon. Elsewhere in this book, I deal at length with techniques for tactfully escalating casual conversations and broaching controversial, delicate, or "hot" topics; however, since learning researchers universally agree that information is processed better when scattered haphazardly throughout a text instead of packaged into easily absorbed, well-defined units, I'd like to mention a few guidelines to keep in mind.

1. Avoid asking strangers where they like to be nibbled.
2. Avoid asking them to confirm their gender.
3. Avoid asking them to confirm your gender.
4. If you ever meet conjoined twins, act like it's the most normal thing you've seen all day.

Why? Why? Why?

You won't find a toddler or a nursing-home resident who doesn't repeat that question hour after hour, day after day. But during the in-between years, we forget all about this critical information-gathering tool. Indeed, I forgot to bring it up until here in the last few sentences of this chapter. Of all the questions you can ask, "Why?" will get you the most thoughtful and expansive responses. Trust me on this. No, don't ask me why. Never, ever ask *me* why.

Anyway, curiosity may have killed the cat, but it will probably spare you. In fact, without it, you'd have little more than shopworn stereotypes to go on. While these may be flawless instruments for judging large groups of people, they aren't nearly as useful one-on-one. But even curiosity will get you only so far. Gathering information is one thing, but really connecting with someone demands that you attempt to see things from that person's perspective, that you be willing to inhabit his or her worldview until you can't hold back your laughter any longer. This utterly alien concept is known as empathy.

Chapter 4

Empathy: Putting Yourself in Someone Else's Ignorant Shoes

The word *empathy* might seem as peculiar to you as *glork* or *zeepie* or *shampoo*. Nevertheless, of all the qualities dealt with in the first section of the book, empathy is by far the one this chapter's about. And what do we mean by *empathy*? Basically, it's the ability to identify with someone else's situation or perspective, to understand what that person is feeling from his or her point of view. Curiosity will help you find out who people are, but you need empathy to help you understand where they're coming from. Empathy ... Fine. It's like what Counselor Troi did on *Star Trek*, but not so intense, okay?

Or maybe you think you already know something about empathy. Like when your team won the World Series, and you and this one guy got the same urge to tear a mailbox from the sidewalk and heave it through the windshield of a squad car. Although this action suggests some sort of viral emotional transfer, that's not what we're dealing with here, per se. But there's another closely related attribute that's sometimes mistaken for empathy, and that, as you might have guessed, is hunger.

Empathy vs. Hunger

It's late at night and rain is pouring down. You're driving along the highway and see a car pulled over, hood propped up, hazard lights flashing. A woman is sitting in the driver's seat, glumly watching the wipers wag back and forth. See if you can distinguish the empathetic response from the hungry one.

> **ELLEN:** Man, I can imagine just sitting there, dwelling on when you'll get to your destination, wondering if that tow truck's ever going to show and whether you should accept help from a stranger. It's a crummy feeling, that sudden helplessness.

> **VICKI:** Did I just pass a Quiznos?

Carefully read the thoughts of each person again. Who seems more likely to be ordering roast beef in the near future? Vicki, of course. But what about Ellen? What's her next move?

Empathy vs. Sympathy

Of all the -mpathies out there, sympathy and empathy are two of the most commonly confused. While empathy refers to identification with someone's situation, sympathy suggests actual participation in someone's feelings. If Ellen not only relates to the stranded motorist's situation but also *feels* it as the motorist does, she's sympathizing, and she may be stirred to assist in some way. But empathy doesn't always lead to sympathy.

> **ELLEN:** It's a crummy feeling, that sudden helplessness. On the other hand, screw her and her right-wing bumper stickers. Let the NRA jump her battery.

Also, be aware that sympathy doesn't necessarily depend on empathy, either. Sometimes people sympathize even if they don't have a true empathetic understanding of the situation. They want to help even though someone's distress is in many ways unfathomable. Let's take, for example, oh, I dunno, you.

> **YOU:** People on the train always say no when I ask them to go to Radio Shack with me. I feel unworthy and unwanted when this happens.

> **SYMPATHETIC LISTENER:** Oh, poor you! I feel terrible about that. I'd be happy to take a trip to Radio Shack with you! Or can I non-sexually comfort you in some other way?

Of course, you can't spell *sympathetic* without *pity me chats*, so you probably have difficulty perceiving the difference between a truly sympathetic listener and one who offers compassion polluted with condescension, otherwise known as pity. Since pity is a corrupted form of sympathy, the two may sound alike in conversation. But someone who pities you usually won't offer genuine assistance, because he hasn't really taken on your suffering.

> **LISTENER WHO MERELY PITIES YOU:** That's really a shame. Poor
> thing. Just let me know if there's anything I can do once I get back
> from my indefinite stay in an underwater city.

Right now you're indignantly trying to tally all the people who promised to e-mail you from Atlantis but never did. Forget them. Now that you understand the difference between sympathy and empathy—now that I'm done talking about it, anyway—you can start using them in your social interactions.

Getting in Touch With Your Inner Someone Else

In the last chapter, I talked about how important listening was, not only for gathering information but also in terms of making someone feel recognized. Your attention will usually be reciprocated, and the mutual interest can congeal into a clumpy, semisolid acquaintanceship. But potential friends want to be understood on a deeper and broader level, in a way that can only be attained through empathy. How do you achieve that?

1. *Try not to judge.* You can't figure out what people are all about if you're constantly condemning them. The safer

someone feels revealing herself, the stronger your connection can be. Look at the exchange below.

> **LISA:** As an adolescent, I often shoplifted bubblegum.
>
> **RON:** There will be no bubblegum in the deepest, darkest, most sulfuric pit of hell. Which is where you're going. I will see to it.

Ron's hurtful attack effectively sabotaged any possibility of a quality relationship with Lisa. But what could he have said?

> **LISA:** As an adolescent, I often shoplifted bubblegum.
>
> **RON:** While I do not condone shoplifting—ultimately, it hurts all consumers—I do realize that adolescence is a period during which young people seek out petty thrills, and I appreciate the context in which your crimes took place. Whether or not you burn in hell for your deeds is an open question.

2. *Stay focused on the other person.* It's important to let people have their say. Sometimes, when we just can't bear to hear a voice other than our own, we try to hurry things along.

> **KATIE:** My family's journey from the killing fields of Cambodia to this quiet Boston suburb is really an amazing survival story and has shaped me in so many ways.
>
> **TRACY:** Right, right. So you make your way to America and everything's eventually fine. Then what?

When we do this, we're signaling to the other person that their thoughts—their very identities—aren't worth our attention and that the only story worth hearing is the one *we're* telling. But sometimes we cut people off not because we aren't interested but because we want to volunteer information about ourselves to indicate a common bond. Our eagerness to empathize, however, actually compromises our ability to do so.

> **KATIE:** My family's journey from the k—
>
> **TRACY:** I know exactly where you're coming from. When we moved to Boston from Connecticut, one of the kitchen boxes got left on the driveway, so we didn't have the juicer for, like, a week.

Of course, hearing people out isn't the same as just sitting there. Actually, I guess it *is* mostly the same, but there's more to it.

3. Facilitate an appropriate environment. Instead of judging or interrupting, you can create an atmosphere in which the person you're with feels welcome expressing himself. One way to do this is with gentle conversational prompts that demonstrate not just your attention but also your willingness to at least comprehend his way of looking at things.

> **NICK:** My wife isn't fair to me.
>
> **SCOTT:** This fact is causing you distress.

NICK:	Yeah. She's constantly getting on my case about money. Always with the nagging. You don't see me accusing *her* of blowing our life's savings on my mistress.
SCOTT:	You wish she'd put herself in your place for once.
NICK:	Exactly. If she would just, you know, open her heart to me, accept me, not be so grossed out by swingers' clubs.
SCOTT:	You are suffering. This is clear.

Notice how Scott varied his language. Though the content of his statements was essentially the same, he didn't come off as dull or mechanical. This is crucial, because the more you repeat yourself, the more you undermine your listener's faith in your attention. And if you aren't paying attention to your words, you probably aren't paying attention to the conversation.

STEPHANIE:	I'd love to go to grad school, but I've still got my undergrad loans to contend with.
MATT:	That's a tough decision, isn't it?
STEPHANIE:	Sure is. I mean, I don't need any more debt, but I could probably earn more with an advanced degree.
MATT:	Yeah, that's tough all right.
STEPHANIE:	I just wish I had a clearer picture of the cost-benefit situation, you know?
MATT:	Tough, real tough.

STEPHANIE:	Hmm … It's like choosing between winning the lottery and skewering your eyeballs.
MATT:	That sure is a tough one.
STEPHANIE:	Butterfly. Gonad. Count Chocula.
MATT:	Wow, that really is a tough situation.

Empathy for the Devil

Sometimes we can draw on our life experiences to empathize with someone. For example, a friend of mine recently described how frustrating it was trying to get through to his uncle with Alzheimer's. Although no one in my family has that terrible disease, I remembered an unproductive conversation I had with an L.L. Bean customer-service representative who insisted there were no hunter-green chamois pajamas in stock—even though the Web catalog clearly said otherwise. On another occasion, I was unable to get a waitress's attention immediately. So, although I couldn't relate to the specifics of my friend's situation, I knew his emotional struggle all too well.

But what if someone's point of view is not only alien in terms of your shared histories but also so bizarre or abhorrent that any kind of rapport seems impossible?

MITCH:	I stole all the toys that were supposed to be given out to needy children on Christmas, pawned them for whatever I could get, then used the money to purchase cigarettes, which I then redistributed to

Quiz: Is Your Empathy Working?

I didn't benefit from empathy as a kid. When I finished second runner-up in the national spelling bee, instead of congratulating me, my mother found a way to work *psittacosis* into every sentence she uttered until I graduated from high school. I remember only two marginal empathetic experiences, in fact. The first was when Blaine Mullin trampled my science-fair project and said, "That must suck for you, dorkhole." The other was when he did it again the following year and said the same thing. As a result, I was late developing empathetic skills of my own, a deficiency best illustrated by the great-aunt/funeral/hula hoop incident of 1994. And even when I tried empathizing, I never paid much attention to what I was doing or the effects my efforts were having. But if empathy is all about attuning yourself to someone else, then you must adjust your approach according to the reaction you get. In each of the groups below, which seems to be the response you're looking for?

    a. "Exactly! You really seem to get where I'm coming from."

    b. "You don't quite understand me."

    c. "Did you just ask me if there was a connection between the passing of my grandmother and the strange fluid leaking from the corners of my eyes?"

    a. Makes direct eye contact.

    b. Distractedly looks out window.

    c. Distractedly looks out window. Jumps.

a. Uses conversational pauses to unhurriedly reflect on his thoughts.
b. Uses conversational pauses to check e-mail.
c. Uses conversational pauses to call second, superior friend

a. Mirrors your body language by leaning forward and gesturing enthusiastically.
b. Mirrors your body language with rigidity or fidgetiness.
c. Mirrors your body language by making a loose fist and pumping it back and forth.

a. Sincerely thanks you for listening to his dating woes.
b. Irritably accuses you of belittling his dating woes.
c. Angrily rejects your attempt to link his dating woes to Al Qaeda.

Your Empathy Index revealed: Give yourself two points for each *a* response, one point for each *b*, and zero points for each *c*.

0	"It rubs the lotion on its skin or else it gets the hose again."
1–4	"Frankly, my dear, I don't give a damn."
5–7	"What we've got here is failure to communicate."
8–10	"Your score on this quiz reflects well-developed empathy skills and a knack for putting yourself in someone else's place, Austin Powers."

those same needy children. I thought it might be funny to watch them getting addicted to nicotine early in life instead of enjoying Christmas like their more privileged peers. And I loved every life-shortening second of it.

If you work for a tobacco company, you're appalled by Mitch's behavior because cigarettes and toys should *never* be an either/or situation for a child. The rest of us think Mitch's behavior is pretty despicable from start to finish. You can't sympathize with him, but maybe you can try to empathize. After all, maybe that's what's been missing from his life from the beginning—and maybe that's what will finally turn him around.

YOU: I bet you had some lousy Christmases as a kid, didn't you, Mitch?

MITCH: No one wants to hear about that.

YOU: Try me.

MITCH: It was 1978, and my mother had just finished baking gingerbread cookies. The first batch was a little burnt on the bottom, not the whole batch but much of it.

YOU: Go on.

MITCH: Anyway, I've spent all the years since that day just lashing out.

YOU: The source of your pain is clear to me now.

MITCH: Thank you for letting me speak my piece without criticism. It's nice to know that someone was willing to spend time reaching out to an obvious sociopath instead of taking steps to succor those he harmed.

YOU: Thanks. Hey, wait a second …

I Flee Your Pain

This concludes the first section of the book and our analysis of your most worrisome deficiencies. Because I can empathize, I know how you must feel: You're proud of having made it this far, but wary of what lies ahead. You're eager to learn from the next section, but you wonder if that will make things awkward between you and the first section when you visit. So, where do you stand? If you've absorbed the first section as you should have, if you've allowed it to displace nonessential information such as your phone number and your awareness of your peanut allergy, you're now the *kind* of person you need to be—but you still lack the tools, my friend. Ability means nothing without them. Wolfgang Amadeus Mozart may have been born with prodigious musical gifts, but, sadly, he discovered the piano far too late in life to ever do very much with them. You, on the other hand, have part two right here waiting, quivering with guidance. It begins the way most brand-new social interactions do: with—no, not a soft kiss on the nape of the neck. Do you remember now why the judge wanted you to read this book? I'm referring to small talk.

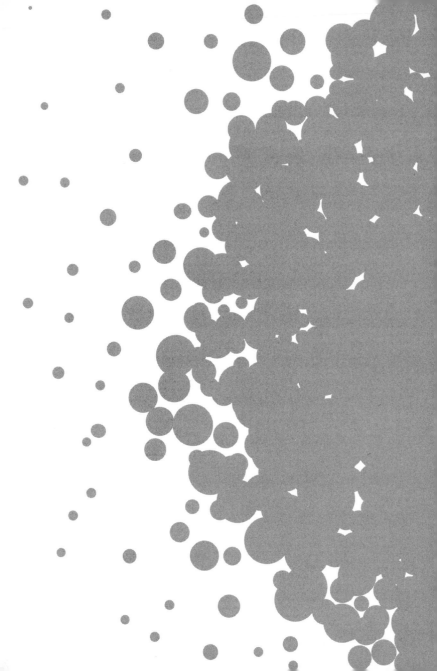

PART TWO!

Conversation for People Who'd Rather Be Home Fondling Their Record Collections, Knitting Berets for Pets They May or May Not Actually Have, or Just Sitting in a Dark Room, Dreaming of an Even Darker Room

Chapter 5

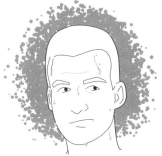

Small Talk: "I Sure Wish This Heat Wave Would End!"

With all due modesty, I'd like to reveal that I was in the gifted-and-talented program throughout grade school. I remember mornings in my standard fifth-grade homeroom, snickering as my classmates began their discussion of the Underground Railroad or the respiratory system. I knew it wouldn't be long before Ms. Nguyen arrived to pull me out of class and conduct me to a room populated by the school's other accelerated learners. There we discussed how certain colors made us feel and were asked, having each been given a picture of a rabbit, to point to the rabbit. (Pointing to the teacher was usually close enough.)

I mention all this because I would like nothing more than to tell you that superior intelligence will see you through. However, important studies in prestigious hardcover journals suggest that in our extroverted society, conversation skills are essential for personal and professional advancement. Oh, sure, maybe you think your nimble hands, composure under stress, and encyclopedic knowledge of the human body will help you achieve your dream of becoming a heart surgeon. But if you can't swap *Family Guy* quotes with a co-worker, just forget it, you valueless nonentity.

Put another way, you know the person sitting next to you on the plane who just cannot get over the fact that his niece once visited the very same megalopolis in which you live? He is your master.

Yes, whether you're trying to meet new friends, make new business contacts, or kill time with a cellmate, you can't get around small talk. And this chapter is here for you.

Before You Begin

I worry you'll interpret the cautions below as a rationale for never risking a conversation. After all, anyone who chronically avoids people by employing excuses such as "But if I go over and say hello, who will stand here and feel utterly disconnected?" is bound to exaggerate any words of warning. Nevertheless, there are three things you need to know up front.

1. Sometimes, the environment does not call for small talk. Under certain circumstances, light conversation should be bypassed.

> **DAVE:** Morning, Wesley. Could you believe that Celtics game? What a disgrace! I'm telling you, Paul Pierce is just carrying that team! I guarantee he'll be asking

for a trade. When are the young guys going to step up and show they're willing to contribute?

WESLEY: (*Engulfed by quicksand.*)

2. Don't barge in. Even in less exigent situations, undertake small talk with care. For one thing, don't insert yourself into an existing conversation without lingering for a moment to get a sense of the tone and content of the exchange.

LIZZIE: I want a baby, and I can't compromise on that. But I love Brandon, and I know how he feels on this matter.

REBECCA: You don't think he'll come around?

LIZZIE: He might. But how long can I wait? I'm already thirty-eight. It's tearing me up.

REBECCA: He loves you. You know that. I—

JOE: Did you guys see *House* last night?

3. Not everyone wants to talk to you. "Oh, really! Thanks for the bulletin. I wasn't debilitatingly aware of that." Please be calm. My general point is that just because someone isn't engaged in a conversation doesn't mean she's necessarily in search of one. Maybe she's preoccupied with something and doesn't want to be distracted. On the other hand, maybe she's perfectly happy to be politely interrupted. How can you tell? Simple. You just find out!

YOU: Sorry for interrupting, but I noticed you were doing one of those Sudoku puzzles. They seem to be all the rage, don't they?

At that point, the person will respond in her own way: "Yes, I normally hate trendy things, but these are so addictive! What sort of puzzles do you enjoy?" or "I'm sorry, but I'm really trying to concentrate" or "Sudoku? I'm feeding ducks, you unobservant fuckup." In any case, what's important is that you were respectful. It's equally important that you handle rejection cordially. We touched on rejection in the first chapter, and if you've forgotten any of the material, now would be a good time to buy a new copy of the book and start again from the beginning.

With the admonishments out of the way, let's begin. Or, as reanimated comedienne Joan Rivers might say, "Can we talk?" (You can add that to chapter two's list of timely pop-culture references.)

Small Talk: Let's Get It Started in Here!

Over the years, CNN's Larry King has persuaded movie stars to open up about how great they get along with their former spouses, athletes to concede that they love their sports, and politicians to admit that they're working in a bipartisan manner to resolve ongoing disputes. So, when a communicator such as this writes a book, even I deign to read it. In *How to Talk to Anyone, Anytime, Anywhere*, King says, "Whether you are at a party or a dinner, on your first day at a new job, meeting your new neighbors, or in any one of a million different settings, the subjects that you can open a conversation with are almost unlimited." Of course, in your case, the phrase *almost unlimited* means they range from "Hi. I collect death-row artwork" to "Excuse me, have you ever tasted turtle jerky?" You should therefore liberally interpret *almost unlimited* to mean "uncompromisingly restricted" and make sure nothing that isn't covered in the list below leaves your mouth.

1. The weather. It's fair to say that no one gets singled out by a blizzard, and that's what's so great about the weather: It's a guaranteed shared experience. And like all good opening topics, it acts as a distant third party that you can praise or criticize as much as you want without risking offense.

> **KEVIN:** They say we'll be having severe thunderstorms all week. I find this a slight annoyance. What is your opinion of this weather?

Kevin is unprovocative enough, yet he discreetly invites the person he's addressing to join him in opposition against a shared foe. Remember that the reason you're bringing up the weather to begin with is because you're trying to establish harmless common ground. Don't overdo it.

> **KEVIN:** They say we'll be having severe thunderstorms all week. Sometimes I just want to choke the barometer until it's sagging in my pitiless hands. The last thing it will hear is me hissing in its ear, "You've postponed your last cookout, goddamn you." What is your opinion of this weather?

2. *A personal observation.* Although discussing the weather is probably the safest approach, making a personal observation will get people talking about themselves faster—there's no third party for them to hide behind. But, for that very reason, personal observations are riskier. You have to be sure that your comment is neither bafflingly vague ...

> **LAEL:** Hi there. You're a male standing in North America.

... nor unnervingly specific.

> **LAEL:** Hi there. You're wearing a suit today, but I can tell you usually don't, because your tie stops an inch and a half above your waistband instead of overlapping your belt buckle. Your truncated sleeves suggest that you should be wearing a 40 long, not a 40 regular, and any clerk with a measuring tape would've told you that if you'd bothered to ask. But you didn't, out of spite. Likewise, you're drinking coffee out of a Styrofoam cup without a lid and you're not taking any precautions with your posture to prevent spillage. You hate this suit because it represents your abandonment of principles you once thought you couldn't live without. Unconsciously, you want to soil yourself. Your father haunts you, doesn't he?

Your best bet is to either offer a mild compliment or ask for a recommendation. Better yet, try to do both! If you're on the rifle range, for example, you could say, "Pardon me, I couldn't help but notice how you outdueled that immobile paper torso. What can I do to become as lethal as you are?"

3. *A situational observation.* Weather, of course, is the best example of a situational observation, but there are many others. Whether you're standing at the bus stop, sitting in a waiting room, or lining up to board Spaceship Earth at Epcot, your surroundings always offer material you can use to strike up a conversation with someone nearby. Imagine that you're on the subway. What might you say to someone in the seat next to you?

- "Can you believe they raised the fares again?"
- "It's stifling in here. I sure wish they'd turn on the air conditioning."
- "That graffito says, 'FLOYD CONTINUOUSLY SUX BALLS.' What's your take on that?"

And remember that your surroundings include not just the physical environment but also the people inhabiting it.

- "This trolley sure is packed. Lucky we got seats!"
- "Gosh, that girl's headphones are really loud, aren't they?"
- "That fellow's schizophrenia makes me smile."

Small Talk: Let's Get It Continued in Here!

I forgot to mention that comments of the sort I discussed in the last section are known as *icebreakers*. Anyway, let's assume you've initiated conversation, and the person hasn't responded with hostility or indifference or a personal-security spray. One thing you can do is volunteer information about yourself in the hope that the other person will follow up with questions of her own. Let's rework an earlier example:

> Gosh, that girl's headphones are really loud, aren't they? I say this despite the fact that I enjoy all kinds of music, everything from Motown to New Wave, and always have it playing—whether I'm driving to my cashier job that I'm using to pay my way through dental school; visiting my parents in my hometown of Cedar Rapids, Iowa; or indoor-rock-climbing with a fellow agnostic vegan who, like me, has experimented with sadomasochism. Pisces.

Did you catch how that icebreaker went beyond observation to providing background on the speaker? The listener now has material to proceed in any number of directions without having to scramble to find something to talk about. This assumes your life has actual content, of course. If you get out less than an agoraphobic under house arrest, you might want to reach for something ready-made.

Current events. Current events can be tricky, because personal views can turn insubstantial small talk into narrow-minded gladiator combat. This might surprise you, given the average American's hunger for varied perspectives. We'll deal with problematic topics in the next chapter, but for now it's best to confine your observations to the marriages, cosmetic-surgery mishaps, and racial tirades of celebrities.

Or you could just mention whatever stupid shit David Blaine is doing.

Sports. I used to spend my Sundays watching the LCC, the Lexus Commercial Channel. It features back-to-back broadcasts of people in mistletoe sweaters surprising each other with luxury cars swathed in elephantine ribbons. Sometimes, the gifts are unveiled semi-creatively, like when the husband finds the car keys at the bottom of his Chardonnay glass, or when the wife wakes up in a windowless room and her husband informs her over an intercom that the key to her Lexus is in the stomach of the unconscious man nearby and that she must choose between not owning a Lexus and burrowing through the still-living man's innards. Anyway, other people watch football on Sundays. And why not? You get action. You get interruptions in the action. You get color commentators offering insights such as "Down by 31, the Redskins need some points on the board" and "I was talking to Darryl before the game, and he's just one of the nicest accessories after the fact you'll ever meet." But just as a blizzard offers more material for conversation than a partly cloudy spring day, underachieving athletes are much more interesting than outstanding ones. Compare.

> **LESLEY:** Can you believe we lost again? I'm sorry, but we really need to clean house!
>
> **KENNETH:** Did you see that play in the fourth quarter? What the hell was the coach thinking? He's just an idiot!
>
> **LESLEY:** We won again. That's seventy-eight in a row. Our dominance continues.
>
> **KENNETH:** Yes. Yes, it does. Did you see that sensible play the coach called in the fourth? Who woulda thunk it? Everyone.
>
> **LESLEY:** Yes. Boo-yah.

Before you bring up sports, try to ascertain if the person you're speaking with will have any interest in the topic. The easiest way to do this is to sneak a peek at the oversize foam finger your interlocutor is wearing. Usually, these souvenirs correspond to a particular sports franchise. Another method would be to use profiling. I *do not* endorse this in any way, however, because a female yoga teacher is just as likely to care about the outcome of the Ultimate Fighting Championship as a man running a cement mixer is.

Hypothetical scenarios. If you're really stuck, you can pose a lighthearted hypothetical question: "If you were on a desert island, what three books would you want?" or "Both of your parents are poisoned, and you have just one

But Enough About Me. Let's Talk About Yoplait: An Alternative to Idle Conversation

Product placement is nothing new in movies. Who could forget how Elliott lured E.T. out of hiding with Reese's Pieces, or that Oskar Schindler always flossed with Glide? Celebrities have been known to transparently shill for specific products in interviews as well, making a mockery of the important questions the *Extra* red-carpet correspondent is asking at the premiere of a movie about computer-animated koalas that say "fo' shizzle" for some reason. But you don't have to be famous to sell out; in fact, advertisers know that, for all their appeal, stars can't always deliver the goods. (For example, Joe Pesci's appearances on *Letterman* did little for Tampax sales.) There's money to be made by everyday folks in everyday chit-chat. But you have to know the rules, and you must not take them lightly. Look how ridiculous the amateur sounds in an exchange with a woman seated next to him on the bus.

WOMAN:	This bus sure is crowded. Lucky we got seats.
AMATEUR:	I wish I had Hot Pockets with me.
WOMAN:	Pardon?
AMATEUR:	Now available in Tangy Sweet-and-Sour Chicken.
WOMAN:	I'm not following you. What's tangy, now?
AMATEUR:	I am, ever since I joined Bally Total Fitness for just $29 a month.
WOMAN:	Are you feeling well?
AMATEUR:	I'm a Mac. And I'm a PC.

Rule 1: Keep It Natural

Be sure your endorsements fit into the conversational flow. For example, imagine you're at the funeral of a distant relative.

WRONG

MOURNER:	Were you close to my uncle?
YOU:	Meow Mix.

CORRECT

MOURNER:	Were you close to my uncle?
YOU:	Well, it's hard to characterize our bond, you know? I always felt a little better, a little happier to be here, after chatting with Joe. It's kind of like how Gatorade replenishes your electrolytes to help you maintain your peak level of performance. And he was so, so generous. Like Old El Paso salsa, his was a thick 'n' chunky soul. If I know Joe, he would have wanted me to share these coupons to Jiffy Lube with those he loved. But unlike Joe, who was embraced everywhere he went, these coupons are void in Alaska and Hawaii.

Rule 2: Connect With Your Audience

Advertisers tailor their messages to particular demographics. You should, too.

WRONG

OLD MAN AT BUS STOP:	We sure got a hot one today. They oughta put a water fountain out here.

YOU: Water's fine, beeyotch, but how about a chuggable Sierra Mist? It's totally pimped out with natural citrus flava.

CORRECT

OLD MAN AT BUS STOP: We sure got a hot one today. They oughta put a water fountain out here.

YOU: Water's fine, except that it wants to take away your driver's license. But how about a Sierra Mist? It's got the lemon-lime taste that respects its elders.

Rule 3: Be Sure the Person You're Talking to Could Benefit From Your Product

WRONG

PRESIDENT OF UNIVERSITY: A newspaper subscription? Naturally, I already have one—several, in fact.

CORRECT

PRESIDENT OF UNITED STATES: I think I'm getting you now. This thing is like alphabet soup, but the noodle letters are on paper and aren't really noodles but printed noodles. Go on …

Putting It All Together

It's Monday morning. Gregarious co-worker Bill is coming 'round to see how things went over the long Fourth of July holiday.

BILL: Hey, chief, have a good weekend?

> **YOU:** Absolutely. Four words, my friend: *Deal or No Deal.* Everyone else was showing reruns, but *Deal or No Deal* was all new with supersized jackpots. Bill, you should have seen this one contestant say the number fourteen. It was electrifying.
>
> **BILL:** Well, my fiancée and I went out to the Cape. We had a lot of fun.
>
> **YOU:** Aren't Carnival cruises great?
>
> **BILL:** I didn't say anything about a cruise.
>
> **YOU:** Oh, you said "a lot of fun." I just naturally assumed.
>
> **BILL:** You go anywhere special?
>
> **YOU:** Is the Kia Summer Sales Event special? I think we both know the answer to that.

dose of antidote. Which one dies? And you have to say it like, 'I want so-and-so to die.'" These come in handy when the entirety of reality just seems like a conversational dead end. Make sure that your scenario poses an ethical dilemma of some sort or compels someone to choose from a number of unsavory options. Just because a setup sounds hypothetical doesn't mean it actually operates that way.

- "You find a magic lamp. You rub the lamp, and a genie materializes. He says, 'What's the capital of Oregon?'"

- "You find a wallet stuffed with money on a park bench. Then you realize it's your wallet, which must've slipped out of your pocket. What do you do?"

- "You get to heaven and Saint Peter wants to know if you'll have sex with me tonight."

Small Talk: Let's Get Out of Here in Here!

All conversations end, of course, even good ones. If you're lucky, you'll find yourself in the unfamiliar position of *choosing* to end a conversation, instead of having it terminated with an awkward excuse or your one and only warning shot.

When withdrawing from a conversation, you have a single objective: to leave a positive impression. Don't give someone any reason to suspect that the tolerable, harmless-enough person he just spent the last ten minutes with was some sort of elaborate façade. When you're ready to move on, go out with optimism and confidence!

Let's assume that Taryn and Diane have been chatting pleasantly for a while, and now Taryn has to head home to touch her front door three times and stand on one foot for exactly eleven seconds to keep the world from ending. Compare these two exit lines.

> **TARYN:** It was really great meeting you, Diane! Best of luck with your new job! Enjoy the rest of the party!

> **TARYN:** It was great meeting you, Diane. You probably found our conversation anguishing. I bet you felt like Job.

And remember that friendship is the ultimate goal. If the person you're speaking with seems like someone you might want to spend more time with, be sure to mention that in your parting words. If you can, propose an activity of mutual interest, and try to be specific with your time frame. Vague plans never seem to happen.

> **TARYN:**   Say, since tennis is an activity of mutual interest, I was wondering if you'd like to play next week—if you're not scared!

If I'm Diane, I'm thinking, "You're on, potential friend!" But how enthusiastic do you think Diane would be if Taryn said the following?

> **TARYN:**   It's easy to find out where you live, so just expect to discover me in your apartment at some point during the next calendar year. One of my hobbies is de-fleaing old rugs. It will be your hobby, too.

Dirty Talk

Gotcha! I wrote that subhead because I knew it would make you pick up this book!

But actually it also makes a point: Conversations sometimes don't proceed as neatly as this chapter would have you believe. No one sees the world in exactly the same way, after all, and it's this diversity that fuels not only our most heinous intercontinental bloodbaths but also our most stimulating conversations.

How do we disagree without being disagreeable? How should we handle problem conversations? What's the best

Memorizing Names Like a Phone Book

I spent much of my early life without a proper name. My birth certificate was never filled in, and because someone set a mug down on it my official name is ring-shaped coffee stain. I'm in the position now, however, where most people know my name; the few who don't quickly succumb to my pheromones and just have to find out. And no one seems to care if I can identify them properly. They'll just say something like "You wouldn't be the first to confuse *Greg* with *you with the unibrow*."

But since you don't have an iota of my magnetism, people won't grant you the same sort of accommodation. There's nothing more disrespectful than forgetting someone's name in the course of a conversation; on the other hand, if you can retain it not just during your conversation but over the course of an evening and beyond, you'll make a great impression.

1. **Repeat the name out loud.** Hearing it in your own voice will help you retain it.

> JAMIE: Hello, Steve. Great to meet you, Steve. Steve, have you been a member at this gym long, Steve? Steve. Steve, Steve, Steve, Steve, Steve, Steve. Steve, I'm ... Oh, crap.

2. **Associate the name with a distinguishing characteristic.** For example, if Teresa is really tall, you can think of her as "tall Teresa." Or if Matt is overweight, you can rhyme his name with *fat*. You can do the same thing if Lockingly Oopid Mattoos has shockingly stupid tattoos.

3. **Memorize the actual name.** If you rely on association, you run the risk of forgetting the name that the helper word was supposed to point you toward. Actually, the name itself is the best mnemonic device of all. It's foolproof. If I meet Corey, the simplest thing to do is retain the word *Corey*. That way, next time I see him, I just think, "Corey," which leads me directly to his name. I'm surprised more books don't recommend this technique.

Despite our best intentions, however, we do lose track of names. Sometimes a person will reintroduce himself without prompting, especially if he's also forgotten your name. But at other times we're not so fortunate. What then? You could apologize and sheepishly admit that his name somehow slipped your mind. He'll usually take your poor memory in stride and banish you from his life without any hard feelings. Or, instead, you could delicately trick him into revealing himself—then act as if you knew all along! In the dialogue below, Josh and Leroy bump into each other on the sidewalk about a month after first meeting at a party.

> **LEROY:** Hi there, Josh. Nice to see you again. How's law school treating you these days?
>
> **JOSH:** We will role-play now. I'm a customer-service representative, and you're calling to have cable installed. Hello, my name is Josh, and this call is being recorded to ensure quality customer service. Could I have your name, sir?
>
> **LEROY:** Um, okay. It's Leroy—
>
> **JOSH:** Oh, hey, Leroy. School's fine. What's up with you?

way to gracefully negotiate loaded topics such as politics, religion, or those puritanical, anachronistic age-of-consent laws written by legislative prudes who think they can just appoint themselves members of the "Sex Gestapo"? You'll find out in the next chapter.

Chapter 6

Difficult People and Topics: "I Sure Wish This Heat Wave Were Being Tortured at a Secret CIA Prison!"

Here's something you might not know but probably suspect by now: I'm in elite physical condition. More than a fifth of the world's aggregate deep knee bends can be attributed to me alone. I also endorse a line of jump ropes. Anyway, a few weeks ago, I was performing squat thrusts when this gentleman I had never met before sauntered over and said that, instead of exercising, maybe I ought to be heeding the word of the Lord. It was bad enough that he hassled me, but here's the irony: *I* was the one who got thrown out of the church. However, now that I've had some time to reflect on the incident, I find myself cornered by a truth I've been loath to own up to: Other people can be uptight and unreasonable. On your quest for friendship, it's only a matter of time before you're also confronted by discourteous people or points of view that differ greatly from your own.

People Are Strange

Those lyrics are most commonly associated with Jim Morrison of the Doors, and you probably know the song even if you're not a fan of classic rock or haven't seen the 1980s biopic starring Iceman. But people *are* strange, not to mention frustrating. If we all walked around in sandwich boards that revealed our inner thoughts, we would know from a distance if a woman disliked her sister-in-law or if a man had fulfilled his dream of wearing a sandwich board. Unfortunately, we usually don't know what we're in for until we've entered into a conversation, and by the time we realize that we're in the presence of somebody we should have avoided, it's too late. But that doesn't mean you're defenseless. Before we look at specific types of undesirables, let's touch on some general strategies for extracting yourself from an unpleasant conversation. Most of you will find these bitterly familiar.

Call upon your biological urges. You usually can't walk away from a conversation without at least some sort of slipshod pretense, and hunger's a good one. If someone's wearing you down with their reminiscences of gift certificates they've received over the years, you can excuse yourself with "I think I'll get myself some of those tasty appetizers" or "Sounds like they're slaughtering additional chickens.

I'm going back for seconds." Unfortunately, all the other person has to do is counter with "Delicious! I think I'll join you" and you're stuck. That's where going to the bathroom comes in. It's an incontestable excuse that begs no follow-up. It's rare that someone declares his intention to use the facilities and in response hears "Really? Are you a big fan of toilets?" or "Delicious! I think I'll join you." Of course, people are generally squeamish about bodily functions. They just don't want to know. If you're worried that your restroom excuse is too transparent, simply concoct something anatomically obscure and unsettling.

- "Hate to cut you off, but my membranes are lathering."
- "Sorry, I need to void my pus nodes."
- "I've been coughing up sussudio all week."

Bring in a third party. Some people are so hungry for closeness that they won't even let you get your name out before presenting you with your half of a heart locket. They exchange poems with prisoners about things like freedom and incompetent public defenders, and they're not 100 percent sure, but they think the person who sent them an e-mail regarding "vigara schoolgirlz who wants 2 gag on your best hippo cock" is probably their soul mate. No rhetorical maneuver will detach these needy people. And yet, you're not really special to them, either. You're just a human who, for the moment, is keeping them from being dragged away in the undertow of their loneliness. You are easily substituted, and you can swap yourself with someone else. If you're at a social function, it's not difficult to find someone else, but you can't just flag down an acquaintance and say, "Listen, Heather, I have to separate myself from this horrible, horrible person. I propose you talk to him." The trick is to make the switch seem beneficial to both the person you've recruited and the person you're retreating from. Then, as they explore their common ground, you can bow out with a clear conscience.

> **ALISSA:** Heather, come here for a second. Remember when you studied Celtic folklore for a year in Ireland? Well, it just so happens that Brad here also spends most of his paycheck on masseuses who are willing to "finish the job." I'll let you two get acquainted. I'm surprised your paths haven't crossed already.

Reinforce the positive. Even if you're with someone who hasn't made the best impression, it helps to end on a supportive note. You never know when you might need a professional contact or want access to someone who really frightens you. You'll score extra points if you encourage the person in terms of something he or she mentioned earlier in the conversation:

- "Well, it was nice meeting you! Thanks for all the unsolicited recipes for placenta."
- "I've really enjoyed our chat! Ecoterrorism seems like a dynamic field."
- "Hey, it's been a pleasure! I'll be sure to pick up that DVD you recommended next time I'm in the mood

to watch people old enough to be my grandparents fuck people old enough to be their grandparents."

Undesirables You Will Encounter and How to Deal With Them

I'm sure you've noticed how resolutely I've avoided generalizations. The last thing someone like you needs is to be reduced to a pitiful caricature. But although you are a singular, beautiful snowflake, other people can be herded into categories based on just one off-putting personality trait. I've even given them funny names.

Billy the Bully. As I'm sure you remember from junior high, high school, college, and this morning, bullies simply want to dominate. Conversational bullies have no interest in making your acquaintance, and they certainly don't want your friendship. All that matters to them is conquest. If the bully had his way, even the most trivial exchange would end with him towering over your trembling body and screaming something like "I told you I enjoyed mystery novels, didn't I, motherfucker!" When I was in kindergarten, my mother told me that the only language bullies understand is airtight logic, particularly if in your argument you use their own words against them but with the grammar corrected. And she was right, actually, but my debating skills were so poor I found myself conceding that anything less than getting repeatedly punched in the face would be unethical. In conversation, you don't have to argue, but you do have to stand firm when confronted.

COLBY:	That concert was spectacular!
JANELLE:	No, it wasn't! What kind of probable child molester says such a thing? You're wrong and should hang.
COLBY:	Well, to each his own. You say potato, and I say potahto.
JANELLE:	Your hackneyed tolerance of the opinions of others has chastened me.

Boris the Bore. Some people don't so much speak as hemorrhage words. They don't care if you find these words relevant or interesting, because what's most important to them is that there be no delay in their recounting of a nonevent. And there will be few pauses for you to work with, because these individuals have learned to breathe through their pupils. They're not arrogant, necessarily, but they're so uncomfortable participating in an actual dialogue that they stick to their scripts. Your job is to throw them off balance when you're finally able to sneak a word in edgewise. The moment you prompt a hesitation, you can make your getaway. For example, let's say your bore is regaling you with a story about a limited warranty he signed up for or a list of all the words that rhyme with *clam.* Even people who breathe through their eyes have to blink, and when they do, you can attempt to short-circuit their minds with "Everything I say is a lie. Is that a lie?" or "David Caruso is employed." You can stun these people for only so long, however, and if you fail to take advantage of your opportunity to escape, you might waste the best years of your life listening to someone describe the choicest parking spots he's ever had.

Narcissus the Nar ... Narca ... Egotist. If you know your Greek myths at all, you know the story of Narcissus, a handsome youth who gazed upon his reflection in a pool and was so smitten, he turned to stone. Indeed, like a statue, narcissists are stuck—on themselves. They will engage in a conversation only to the extent that it gratifies their egos and will find a way to convert any information into a rationale for self-praise.

> **SHANA:** We decided that it was better to put Trixie to sleep than to put her through the ordeal of surgery. Even if she survived, she likely wouldn't have much of a life. Actually, the worst part was the way she shook when we put her in the animal carrier, like she knew what was coming.
>
> **VICTOR:** That reminds me of the time I did sixteen one-armed pull-ups.

Some narcissists will let people come and go, because they barely notice that anyone else is there to begin with. Others will chafe at any effort to withdraw from their company, because they don't think anything could be more worthwhile than spending time with them. In the latter case, you can use their vanity to your advantage:

JUDY: You know, I can't get over the extent to which I'm savoring our face-to-face conversation, but I was wondering if you'd turn around for a while. I'd like to give your buttocks the long, unhurried look they deserve.

She Who Walks on the Wind With the Raven Spirit the Cynic. The cynic wants to infect you with her contempt for the hideous, selfish phonies she wishes would let her into their lives. Your sole function in a conversation with this person is to agree that certain things are total bullshit. Cynics are as angry as bullies but don't have the intimidation chops. They can be knocked down with the *threat* of a feather. But the cynic is potentially more dangerous, long term. If you linger in her presence, you will be contaminated. You'll see a mother nursing her newborn child and think, "Typical." Fortunately, cynics are easy to break away from, whether you manufacture an excuse or just duck behind some curtains. They expect nothing less of you.

The Anonymous and Unloved Burden on Society Who Hasn't Purchased This Book. Actually, you probably won't find yourself in a conversation with this sort very often. The stink would be unbearable.

Handling Difficult Topics Gracefully

They say that death and taxes are the two subjects you should always avoid in polite conversation, but I've discovered firsthand that even the most respectful observation about minors and abortion can totally spoil the vibe in a conga line. We're all sensitive about something, and though we can't identify everyone's personal triggers—how can we know at a glance that someone might be touchy about his mindless job or the scar that zigzags across his face like the tracings of an EKG?—we as a culture tend to freak out about politics and religion, in particular. Navigating these topics in conversation requires that you find common ground. This might seem unimaginable, given the contentiousness surrounding these topics, but if your mind and heart are generous, you'll find that what you dismissed as "unimaginable" is actually "negligibly possible, but not at all realistic."

Politics. As I write this, Democrats are just weeks away from officially taking control of Congress, and both they and the Bush administration have promised to work as partners to move the nation forward. Although I'm confident this historic pledge will usher in a utopian society, there's always the remote possibility that the parties involved won't follow through and that politics will remain as divisive as ever. But don't forget that, however we vote, we're *all* Americans— and if you don't forget, neither will other people.

> **JARED:** I hate looking out the window when I'm stuck at home sick. It just makes me think of all the drilling I could be doing in the Arctic National Wildlife Refuge.

ELLIE:	Like you, I'm concerned about how our country will meet both its short- and long-term energy demands. But there's no reason all Americans can't come together on this issue. Look, we *all* need energy, right?
JARED:	You speak the truth. I look forward to draining Lake Michigan with you.

Religion. It's a shame that in a country with freedom of religion enshrined in the very first amendment to its constitution there are still some people who haven't accepted Jesus as their Lord and Savior. But, until that day arrives, the place of religion in public as well as private life will always be up for debate. The thing to remember is that no one, neither the devout believer nor the buzz-killing atheist, really knows how it all began.

CONNIE:	I had just left the bakery the other day when I thought to myself, "If you believe in God, you must be some sort of imbecile man-child."
ROB:	Like you, I'm just looking for answers, trying to make some sense of this cosmic mystery called life. I'll admit that the world tests my faith sometimes, and I'm really not the narrow-minded zealot you think I am.
CONNIE:	Ooh, does that mean you're going to put a voodoo curse on me?

Gay marriage. This issue gets special mention because nothing—not even an actual election—drives voters to the ballot box quite like gay marriage. After all, what could be more transgressive than wanting to participate, as billions of others have, in one of civilization's most ancient institutions? It's important to realize that all of us, no matter where we stand on this issue, have the position we do because of the high regard we have for matrimony. You can use that to build bridges.

> **MALCOLM:** If we let a man marry another man, what's to stop him from marrying his brother or his father or his basset hound? "Hey, look at me, I'm gay and just got back from my honeymoon with my refrigerator."
>
> **JANET:** Like you, I cherish the—wait, what in the name of fuck are you talking about?

Set the Word on Fire

If I were to ask you what you do when you meet someone for the very first time, you'd probably tell me that you say hello or beg for a lock of hair. That's because when you think of communication, you most likely think of verbal language, overlooking the fact that there's lots of information we transmit without a sound. Our faces and bodies send messages of their own, and if we don't pay attention to them they can undermine what we're trying to achieve with our words. We may vocalize the sentence "Hello! Is this your first time in an improv class?" but our gloomy visual cues may be saying, "Do you know when Dr. Kevorkian's getting out of prison?" On the other hand, if we work with our bodies, we can project a totally different image, one that says, "Hi! I'm confident, optimistic, and unarmed. Let's chat." So stand up straight and shake hands with the next chapter.

Chapter 7

Nonverbal Communication: Are You and Your Nostrils on the Same Page?

Nonverbal communication is something so important it could only be buried three-quarters of the way through this book. Consider mimes, for example. It can hardly be a coincidence that their complete reliance on body language coincides with their enduring popularity. Why is this so?

For one thing, spoken language as we know it hasn't always existed. The archaeological record of the early hominids is crystal clear. For millennia, a question was answered by choking unconscious the person posing it, though few of these answers were ever given, because questions were asked the same way. Subsequently, our ancestors developed a slightly more sophisticated method of communication: Let a mastodon trample you to death once for no, twice for yes. With well-earned extinction approaching, we finally learned to point at our genitals, and that turned out to be all we needed. (Though we can't imagine living without it, language only evolved as a way to standardize spelling bees.) The point to remember is that humans are hardwired to communicate physically.

Second, we usually see people before we hear them. This is not always the case, of course—maybe you've been chatting over the phone with your soon-to-be-morbidly-disillusioned Internet date, or maybe you just can't figure out how to get the pillowcase off your head. But, generally speaking, if you project the wrong visual cues, you may not even get the chance to demonstrate your verbal incoherence. And by *visual cues*, I'm not necessarily referring to appearance—wardrobe, haircut, and such. (However, frat boys who wear tiny beaded medicine pouches around their necks should be shunned pretty much immediately.) I'm talking about gestures, the things you can *do*. In the classier social sciences, these are known as *interkinetic signifiers*. There are a number of these, presented here in the order I jotted them down along the perimeter of a Chinese restaurant's horoscope place mat.

Smiling

While there isn't a person alive who isn't intimately familiar with the 1986 David Lee Roth album *Eat 'Em and*

Smile, we don't often sit down and consider what it really means to smile. When you pass someone on the street and the tight crease of her lips twitches in fleeting and reluctant acknowledgment of your existence, is that a smile? When a disgraced congressman flashes his veneers for his mug shot, or when a beauty-pageant contestant grins through her pledge to dedicate every ribbon-cutting ceremony and 4-H livestock auction to the women of Sudan, are they truly smiling? Technically, yes. But for socializing you need something more, something relaxed, friendly, genuine. I don't think I need to remind you where you stand in terms of these qualities, so what you're tasked with is manufacturing a smile that's sincere, a welcoming expression that masks your many inner resentments and makes people think, "Yep, that right there's a stable non-asshole."

Your best course of action here—like just about everything I've recommended in the book to this point—couldn't be more obvious. Simply form a mental picture of a happy memory (sangria with my friends on Nantucket last summer), an exciting ambition (youngest executive vice-president in the firm's history), a funny deformity (like when three fingers are sort of fused into one giant Twinkie finger), or something else that makes you smile. And by *smile*, I mean only that. If your mental picture also causes you to giggle, drool, or pantomime knife sharpening, you will get nowhere.

Of course, if it's true that you're never fully dressed without a smile, the opposite also holds ... Actually, the opposite is nonsensical. Maybe I should just talk about eye contact.

Eye Contact

Come to think of it, this is probably the most important element of successful body language, so I hope you remembered to read this section first. Noses and elbows are just parts—only the eyes allow you to confront the essence of a person. It's easy, then, to see why someone like you would rather look over someone's shoulder at the flat-screen TV broadcasting arena football than engage in eye contact: You're afraid of being exposed. You worry that one look at your pupils will show a person all she needs to know about your shameful inhalant addiction/yakuza ties/humor book. Or maybe your fears aren't so specific. Maybe you're just scared of being revealed, not as the riddle wrapped in a mystery you pretend to be, but as the simpleton wrapped in obesity you actually are. Nevertheless, the human connection you so desperately crave is probably out of the question unless you're willing to look someone right in the eye and— well, do that. (See "The Rule of Four FAQ"—which you probably read before any of this body text, anyway—for more information.)

The Rule of Four FAQ

Hello!
Um, hello.

What is this thrilling tool?
The Rule of Four provides a template for those who struggle with sustaining eye contact. It's simple enough: Hold eye contact to a count of four, look away briefly, then resume and repeat. That's it. It's as perfect as it is great.

Now that's a discovery! I bet Galileo feels like a real pussy. And you're just giving it away to anyone in the whole world who buys your book?
Can you believe it?

Is there anything I should know about the Rule of Four before I start bettering myself with it?

1. Do not count out loud.
2. Do not look at your watch to count off the four seconds you're supposed to be spending looking at the other person.
3. If the eyes have nipple rings, they are not eyes. That's all you need. Now get out there!

Actually, I was wondering: If the other person is wearing an eye patch, should I look at him for twice as long—or for half as long?
Well, I guess the respectful thing to do would be to cover one

of your own eyes with your hand and apply the Rule of Four as usual.

Also, instead of looking away after four seconds, can I just hold my gaze but raise and lower a small velvet curtain?
Odd question here. I mean, I—

Recently, I was on a barge. I spent a couple of minutes chatting with a woman and using the Rule of Four to sustain eye contact. Unfortunately, I never got her name, and I was wondering if you happened to know it. She had a Betty Boop tattoo.
Look, we're getting way off topic here.

Now, just to clarify, this "four" you keep mentioning is some sort of futuristic three, right?
It's four. I mean, come on, four is four.

Why didn't Tarzan fall from the tree?
What? I don't know, I—

Di-vine intervention!
Please don't tell Tarzan jokes in my FAQ.

I have one more question about the Rule of Four: Would you like to buy some Girl Scout cookies?
Why did I make my FAQ an actual interview?

Hello!
I think we're done here.

Nodding

You're most familiar with nodding as a kind of semiconscious gesture used to hold your place in a conversation while you slip away into a personal void or into fantasies in which your nakedness is something sought after by unattainable people. (This type of nodding, a full up-and-down motion, is not to be confused with the half-nod, which is the cheerless tilt of the chin that a suburban adolescent might employ upon encountering one of his homeys at the Rainforest Café.) When combined with active listening, nodding is a great way to reinforce positive verbal interaction. On the other hand, there is danger in nodding inattentively just to get through a conversation—the other person might misinterpret your mechanical acknowledgments as rapt attention and sincere agreement. I'm reminded of an encounter I had with a neighbor years ago. He was dull as could be, but, at the time, I was too timid to break off a conversation. I just absently nodded for an hour or so. Finally, my neighbor said, "I'm so glad we see eye to eye on these matters. I'll just be a sec." He left and returned shortly thereafter with the toaster I apparently agreed to repair and the Christmas lights I apparently agreed to hang. He told me to give him a shout when I was done, and then we'd work out a convenient time to mutually masturbate. My lack of attention cost me, and even now I'm not entirely sure of everything I committed myself to. Sometimes I'll see my neighbor walking up my driveway. He'll be wearing hockey gear or leading a bear cub on a leash or pushing a wheelbarrow filled with glitter. And when I answer the door, he always says the same thing: "You ready?"

Posture

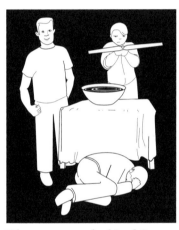

Who wants to make friends?

So far, this chapter on nonverbal communication hasn't dipped below the neck. But effective nonverbal communication requires you to coordinate your whole body. Look at the scene on the left. Which of those people is ready for a conversation? Who would you feel comfortable introducing yourself to? As you can see, we communicate an awful lot with our stance, particularly with our arms. Open arms suggest that you are receptive to conversation; folded arms suggest that you're defensive, unfriendly, or prepared to grant three wishes. Talking with a hand in front of your mouth suggests shyness, propping your head on your hand suggests preoccupation, and planting a hand on your hip suggests anger—all three at once suggests an absolutely enthralling mutation.

Also, leaning toward someone indicates that you are really and truly paying attention. You're saying to him, "Your anecdote, about the immigrant cab driver whose English was almost insufficient for him to convey you to the sterile bistro where all appetizers have been reclassified as *tapas* and where any mixture served in a cocktail glass, including vodka and Crunch Berries, is called a *martini*, is so engrossing I worry that if I don't close the distance between us, someone else—or maybe even a hawk—will swoop in and snatch up your words." But how close is too close? A person's culture will, in part, influence what he or she considers a comfortable social distance, and this is a topic I intend to gloss over in full in the next chapter. For Americans, however, there really isn't a formal rule, though if you're close enough for your eyelashes to get tangled up or cannot only hear but can also inhale the conversation you're having, you're too close. That doesn't mean there isn't a place for actual physical contact, however. And that place is the following section.

Physical Contact

Touching, when used judiciously, is a great way for people to comfortably bridge both physical and emotional space. If you're reading this book, however, physical contact has probably been a long-standing issue for you, either because you fear it or because you've provoked the fear of it in others. How can you identify the *tactile aura* of a situation?

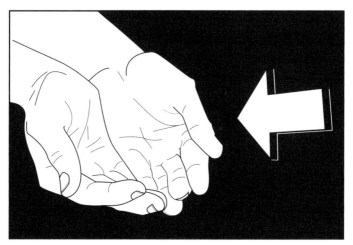
"Hands"

What's actually appropriate in a casual encounter? (In this context, *casual encounter* refers to a purely platonic social interaction, not to the kind of no-strings Internet rendezvous you so often chuckle at and inquire into.) For one thing, a handshake is appropriate just about anywhere.

Shaking hands

Before you put your paw out to anyone, you should completely internalize the following rules.

Memorize the exact location of your hands. When the time comes for the big greeting, you don't want to be scrambling around.

Put a little strength into your grip. Otherwise, it's like shaking hands with lettuce.

But don't squeeze with all your might. I say this not because you don't know your own strength but because the other person probably won't. The viselike grip you imagined yourself to have is actually more like the dainty grasp of a vending-machine claw that can't elevate a five-ounce stuffed toucan more than an inch. Spare yourself this humiliation.

Remember to let go. There's not much transition time between shaking hands and holding hands. You'd be surprised how quickly you can go from "How do you do?" to knowing what Mace tastes like. Usually, a couple of up-and-down arm motions will do the trick. (Modest ones. You are not cracking a whip.)

Don't bring the back of the person's hand up to your face and stroke it against your cheek while cooing, "Your hand is so soft, like an angel's wing." If I have to explain this to you, I cannot explain this to you.

Since people typically shake with corresponding hands, you might find it difficult to practice these rules on your own. I recommend filling a latex glove with warm water and pretending you're introducing yourself to it at a dinner party. It sounds creepy, but if you're actually doing it, it's probably only the fourth-creepiest thing you'll do that day. (Also, I've found that a surprising number of my readers own mannequins. Though their hands are a bit more rigid and a bit less lifelike than the fluid-filled gloves, they will do in a pinch.)

Hugging and kissing

It used to be that a handshake was all you needed. It was how a conversation began and ended, how children were conceived, how milk was delivered. But we now live in more casual times. Ours is an age in which you can't check your coat without some fellow trying to spoon with you. People with natural social skills made appropriate adjustments; others (you are others) failed to do so and were some of the very first people to be served with class-action restraining orders. When's the right time to give a non-intimate hug? When should you venture a peck on the cheek?

Gender is key here. If you're a woman, you generally don't run the risk of offending someone by being affectionate. You should be aware, however, that certain men live according to that well-known dictum: Whatever doesn't kill me is flirting. With these men, the hugs you gave absolutely everyone as you left the party were somehow theirs and theirs alone and will inspire scores of presumptuous and subliterate follow-up text messages ("I rlly enjoyd r date!!! :)"); should you kiss one of these men on the cheek, you can expect a picture of his penis to arrive within half an hour.

On the other hand, if you, the reader, are a male and the sort who has nothing but contempt for the pigs who can't even wait the traditional forty-five minutes before transmitting nude pictures of themselves, you're probably squeamish about being mistaken for one of them. This is easily avoided. Once you've hugged a woman, simply reassure her by saying, "That meant less than nothing," or "Don't worry. I find you plain," or "Your touch was like the touch of a ghoul." There will be no mixed messages and no hurt feelings, just two people who know exactly where they stand.

Summary and Clumsy Shift to New Material

People are like billboards. This analogy is imperfect, of course, because billboards are generally less preoccupied with advertising. Nevertheless, it cannot be denied that we constantly broadcast messages with our bodies about who we are and how we feel. The more attention you devote to smiling, eye contact, nodding, posture, appropriate physical contact, and dragon (sorry, I went too far on the Chinese horoscope place mat), the less attention others will devote to the gibberish issuing from your mouth.

Okay, so that's that. New topic. Now we leave our familiar social landscape and poke our torches into the shadowy nether-realm known as almost the entire world. Let's talk about foreigners.

Chapter 8

Effective Cross-Cultural Communication: Dealing With the World's Five Billion Seven Hundred Million Outsiders

Depending on whom you ask, the United States is a "melting pot" or a "salad" or "a great big jar of jellybeans, some of which were poured in as slaves." It turns out, however, that our facile metaphors don't always reflect the realities of our everyday lives. We wall ourselves off by race, by ethnicity, by ... Well, I mean, those are the biggies. With all the diversity we have at our disposal, we keep looking for ways to subdivide into smaller and smaller comfort zones. Soon our left eye will be wondering if our right eye has the, you know, "values" it wants in a neighbor. Considering all the self-segregation at home, is it any wonder that we Americans struggle so much when introduced to people from foreign countries?

There are other reasons, of course. For one thing, the U.S.—with the exception of a few widely dispersed enclaves and an occasional Florida—is an English-speaking nation, and since English is the language of international communication, we presume that the Sicilian fishmonger picked some up in school or while conducting shuttle diplomacy. We're all to some degree susceptible to this assumption, and some of our countrymen can be obnoxious about it. But most of us realize how lucky we are to have foreigners address us in our native tongue, and when our tour guide says, "How are you enjoying your vacation?" we might good-naturedly correct her—"It's actually '*Whom* are you enjoying your vacation?'"— or let it slide. However we handle it, it's undeniable that languages offer insights into the cultures of the people who speak them, and that by sticking with English we're missing out on learning the arbitrary gender articles for tens of thousands of words.

Also, the reach of our culture is a source of both fascination and resentment—no one makes blockbuster movies or drops A-bombs quite like we do—and generates an ambivalence that hangs in the air any time Americans and non-Americans interact. More on this later, energy permitting. But many of you now are probably thinking, "Hey, I've never been abroad. The only time I've even left my area code was when they changed the area codes. I'm intimidated by accents other than American and high elf, and am suspicious of the agendas of most time zones. So, to add all that to my pre-existing social anxiety seems a little unfair.

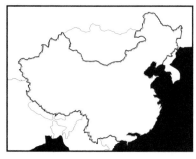
"When asked to identify this country, 93 percent of Americans said, 'The President?'"

I'm still trying to get through some of life's most basic social exchanges. Do you know how humiliating it is to have a transaction at a drive-thru window end with the voice over the intercom saying, 'Honey, is there someone you can call?'"

I understand your situation, but you need to face certain realities. The first reality is that I have a book to fill up in a short amount of time. (If you think the text in this chapter isn't relevant, you might want to bypass the upcoming photos of oversize dolphins.) The second reality is that in this day and age, and more so now than ever, our world is a magnificent tapestry of nations. Satisfied? Now that I've given you some perspective, let's meet our next subhead.

Stereotype—or Stereohype

I just looked it up to double-check, and the word is *stereotype*, not *stereohype*. Anyway, at the end of Chapter 3, I described stereotypes as "flawless instruments for judging large groups of people." As wrong as you were for reading those words— twice now—I, as their author, must also accept some share

Effective Cross-Cultural Communication

of the blame. In any case, they are *not* flawless. Even though some people argue that there's a dash of truth behind even the ugliest stereotypes, my publisher's senior marketing rep has informed me, in an e-mail flagged "Urgent," that I don't agree in the slightest. But it's a fact that Americans, like everyone else, are stereotyped. Although we're greatly admired for some of our achievements—our Constitution, our chicken-fried steak—the complaints against us tend to fall into certain categories.

Americans are ignorant. The extent to which most Americans are unfamiliar with the laws and history of their own country has been well documented, most recently in books such as *The Civics Gap: The Rising Cost of an Uninformed Populace* and *Folks, You're Not Going to Believe How Many People Can't Name Even One Fucking Supreme Court Justice.* And, really, we don't need much information to get through our everyday existence. We're safe and prosperous; our text messages get through pretty reliably. It should come as no surprise, then, that we're even less acquainted with the goings-on in other countries. What little knowledge we have of the rest of the world we've picked up only because of its significant impact on the United States: The 9/11 hijackers trained in Afghanistan, Steve Irwin was from Australia, and Iraq, of course, is where our soldiers are bogged down watching representative democracy blossom. And that's why people from other cultures often consider Americans woefully self-absorbed. No one expects us to know everything,

Effective Cross-Cultural Communication

Bad Libs: Avoiding the Unmentionable in Casual Conversation

Sure, you could spend weeks and months researching the history of a country on the Web or in (*giggle*) a library. Then I guess you could memorize bits of important information or scribble little reminders to help you out. ("Note to self: Do not mention apartheid or shocking rape statistics unless party host mentions them first.") Or you could just fill in the blanks below for your country of choice and take a copy of this page with you on your travels.

1. The defeat of the _____ army by the _____

(indigenous military)   (invading military)

   army continues to be a source of national shame.

2. The infamous regime of _____ was marked by

(despot)

   shortages of _____, widespread _____, and

(good or service)   (type of trauma)

   summary _____.

(type of harsh legal measure undertaken without pesky legal niceties)

3. The disaster at _____ is considered by most

(site of environmental catastrophe the government says you're totally imagining)

   _____ residents to be responsible for widespread

(afflicted region)

   _____ and a generation born without _____.

(chronic pulmonary disease)   (appendage/organ)

4. The collapse of the _____ economy forced once-
(nationality)

prosperous citizens to sell their _____ or to
(type of valuables)

_____ American sex tourists.
(degrading act)

5. _____ vastly underestimated the leopards.
(name of official in charge of monitoring leopards)

but there's no excuse for mistaking the Northern Renais-
sance for a WNBA franchise.

If you know you'll be interacting with someone from a
different country, you can prepare for your encounter with
a little research. Not only will this puncture your stereotypes but it can also help you steer clear of taboo subject
matter. A certain amount of ignorance can be overlooked,
but there are topics that will doom you on contact. For
more information, see "Bad Libs: Avoiding the Unmen-
tionable in Casual Conversation."

Americans are obsessed with careers and money. My
success as a motivator has brought me a certain amount
of material comfort. In the U.S., everyone's impressed
when I cut the line in the best restaurants by slipping
the maître d' a jeweled chariot, but I quickly discovered
that those kinds of displays are regarded as unbecom-
ing in many foreign countries. That's because Americans

Oh, the Humanity!

typically measure success in terms of accumulation of wealth or advancement in a career, while people from other cultures often judge success by one's overall quality of life. That's why that standard American icebreaker "What do you do for a living?" can receive such an aloof reception when used abroad, particularly if the person you're asking is unemployed. Instead of imposing your nation's values on the conversation, respect those of the other person. For example, you could open a conversation with "Do you make jellied eels at home?" or "What's it like to nap so much?"

Americans lack modesty. The United States is the home of casual Friday, which for decades has been corporate America's way of saying, "For the sake of morale, we're going to tone down the dress code! It's been a long week, so what the heck! Consider this your holiday bonus indefinitely." In many countries, the thought of wearing jeans to the office, even just one day a week, is unheard of. In fact, our looseness is sometimes misinterpreted as, well, looseness. Everyone knows we gave the world *Playboy* and the silicone breast implant, and, though we certainly weren't the world's first pornographers, for sheer volume and variety of sex acts burned onto DVD, we rule the planet. But, in a much more general sense, Americans' relative lack of inhibition sometimes sends the wrong message. In other words, nothing says "I want to fuck all of Rome" quite like an ordinary American coed saying the word *hello*. If you're a woman, be aware that

Oh, the Humanity!

your nationality alone might be viewed as an invitation; if you're a man, you can always hope.

Americans do not respect hierarchy. Although Americans might privately be touchy about our country's stratified society, we at least adopt a pretense of equality, of shunning obvious status markers: We call each other by first names most of the time, even in many business contexts, and we use affectionate nicknames—Tiny, Butch, Machine Larynx Instead of Real One—to create a sense of camaraderie. We don't have a formalized caste system, just a lot of poor people who live far away, near subway stations we never stop at, and we don't venerate our elders to the extent they do elsewhere. (You know that rec room at the home, where the Cab Calloway record has been skipping for three hours, and where your grandfather waits for the nurse's aide to get back from hawking his Purple Hearts for OxyContin? Not veneration.) Although Americans really don't see what the big deal is about old people, we do consider women to be full equals, a perspective best demonstrated by the fact that women now earn salaries that verge on coming close to approximating *exactly* what men earn for the same work.

Generally speaking, it's important that you recognize that some cultures operate under a pecking order that you might find unusual. If you're unsure about what dynamic is in play in a group, just pay careful attention. Who seems assertive? And who seems more deferential? Are you picking up any "subjugation vibes"? Do you notice anything that might be a token of status, maybe a special item of jewelry, an important-seeming mustache, or thirty-seven wives? If you can't figure out the hierarchy by observing, don't be afraid to tactfully say, "Pardon me, but which are the unclean people?" The only thing you have to lose is your lack of understanding.

Americans are obsessed with time. What would we do without our day planners! It seems like there isn't a single minute of the day that isn't earmarked for some meeting, activity, or prime-time game show. While some countries share our concern for spending time in the most productive and least reflective ways possible, others do not. People from these latter cultures don't perceive time as something to be carved up into hour long increments, but as a kind of ellipsis you live in. In these countries, planes take off when they feel like it and 2003 hasn't begun yet. These people aren't trying to be rude. They just have a more expansive view of time, one that makes greater accommodations for family life and midday alcohol. When traveling in these cultures, try to get by on local time. Instead of peeking at your atomic clock every thousand billionth of a second, try relying on less precise cues. For example, if you look in the mirror and notice you've visibly aged, you know it's time for breakfast.

Americans are preoccupied with hygiene. Yes, we all know that certain countries don't use deodorant, but it wasn't until I began traveling overseas regularly that I actually realized how wide the divide was. In Spain, for instance,

Oh, the Humanity!

your host will be offended if you bring your own specially sanitized napkin, silverware, food, and table to the dinner table. In Namibia, it's actually considered impolite to pump antibacterial soap into your coffee, and if you merely cringe when a Ukrainian tries to shake your hand, your conversation's pretty much over. The truth is that you'll travel only as far as your tolerance of filth will take you. I know I'm not the only American whose first thought upon seeing the Great Wall was "That can't stop the germs. Nothing stops the germs."

The New Body Language

I've already devoted an entire rip-roaring chapter to body language, and while you couldn't possibly have—though you definitely should have—mastered it by now, I have to confuse you with some contradictory information. It seems that different cultures have different tendencies when it comes to nonverbal communication, and until the various translations of this book eliminate them one by one, you'll just have to adapt accordingly when you encounter them. The good news: The fact that you're reading this book suggests that you have pre-existing issues with nonverbal communication that might serve you well among non-Americans. Take speaking distance. You probably stand either conjugally close or blocks away, hiding in a tree. But, either way, you're better off than most of your fellow countrymen when among certain nationalities.

Oh, the Humanity!

That's because what ordinary Americans might consider too close is perfectly normal among South Americans, for instance; and, similarly, what we might consider an isolating distance is just right among people from many Far Eastern countries. See? It turns out, all you need is a plane ticket, a passport, and an assortment of painful vaccinations, and you'll feel right at home.

I also talked about eye contact earlier. (You'll recall your gratitude upon reading "The Rule of Four.") Americans have a high tolerance for eye contact, which means that if your unbroken stare unsettles your compatriots, it's sure to make a Japanese person combust. But if you're the type whose inability to hold eye contact has caused people to label you as "untrustworthy," "shifty," or a "raving optophobe," you can take heart in knowing that your tendency is regarded as modest and respectful elsewhere. (And I'm strictly referring to *that* tendency. Your many others remain troublesome, even in countries you didn't think would be so uptight.)

Your Ticket Home—and a New Adventure

It's time to leave foreign countries behind and return to Earth. But don't unpack so fast: There's another "ship" for you to catch! This "ship" doesn't travel the high seas, though, and no one's ever vomited all over its shuffleboard deck. This "ship" doesn't ram icebergs or stage fan cruises where passengers get to mingle with the cast of

ALF. This "ship" never weighs anchor—but it can take you all around the world. That's right, in the next section, you'll be departing first class on the *S.S. Friendship* ... Actually, third class. Some other self-help types booked reservations, like, a year in advance. Most of you will have to bunk in the furnace room.

PART THREE!

Making Friends That Last a Lifetime

(or Until Things Just Kind of Drift)

Chapter 9

How Do I Know If Someone's My Friend?

Quick, what's the best present you ever received? Chances are you're thinking of an impressive object—maybe a baseball bat autographed by your favorite player or a new car. (Or, if you want to be a lame-o who says, "My kids," go right ahead.) But there's no gift quite like friendship. In fact, the only gift I give out during the holidays is a small card on which I write, "This Card Entitles the Bearer to One Year of Faithful, Dedicated Friendship." Some people don't appreciate it at first. They say, "So, can I redeem your friendship at Best Buy?" or "What else should I expect from the man who gives out smiles and firm handshakes to trick-or-treaters?" or simply "I wanted what your enemies got." But clothes go out of fashion, video-game consoles become obsolete six months after they're released, and money will only be devalued by inflation. Friendship is different. Whether you choose to renew it annually, as I do, or hold onto it for a lifetime, there's nothing quite as special as being offered someone's friendship. For most people, life just isn't complete without friends, real ones, not the kind who lob cans of Mountain Dew at each other in commercials. But what *is* a friend, really? What's an acquaintance? Why should you even bother? Don't worry, you'll get by with a little help from this chapter.

Friendship Defined and Overexplained

As of this moment, as you read these very words, how many people in your life would you consider friends? Lots, you say? Now I want you to go back and remove from your list any customer-service representative whom you've supplied with the last four digits of your Social Security number. Hey, where'd they all go? See, friends aren't just people who happen to possess some personal information about you. So, you can also exclude the exiled Nigerian cabinet minister to whom you sent your bank's routing code—unsolicited—and the FBI profiler who has devoted six years to identifying your psychosexual motives. Friendship is a *relationship*, and the only way you'll ever develop an authentic friendship with someone is if you first grasp what such a bond entails. What's a friend supposed to do?

A friend puts up with your flaws. We all blow it sometimes. But that's why pencils have erasers and why parents redirect their love toward their second child. A friend doesn't expect you to be perfect. Even when others tell her that you're "a little weird" or "not quite right" or "that person who was on the news," she just chuckles. That's because the virtues you possess far outweigh the defects she's aware of; in fact, if you *didn't* walk around with cotton candy stuck in your hair, well, you just wouldn't be you.

A friend encourages you. A friend wants you to succeed. If you run the Boston Marathon, a friend will cheer you on along your route and will be waiting at the finish line with one of those tinfoil blankets. (And, because she tolerates your flaws, she'll overlook the fact that it took you two hours longer than expected and that you're wearing a lobster bib.) A friend will help you rally the courage to introduce yourself to that cutie at the bar and will help restore your confidence when it dawns on you that 1-800-GO-NAVY is not her cell number.

A friend is honest with you. Maybe you're not equipped for the Boston Marathon. Maybe you're delusional about your readiness, explaining that you'll just get your sneakers and gastric bypass on the way to the starting line. A *true* friend would tell you he thought you were making a mistake, even if it strained your relationship. But that's difficult to appreciate sometimes, especially from people we count on for a boost. Actually, I sent copies of this very book to three of my closest friends and urged them to hit me with their truthful opinions. One friend said, "Well, I love how this book isn't a choking hazard." Another said,

"Amazing! Every word just seems printed right there on the page!" (I still haven't heard from the third friend. He said he had read the book but that he wouldn't have time to chat about it until he returned from Oklahoma. I wasn't aware of this, but apparently he's a rodeo-clown reservist and was called up for active duty.) Sure, my friends were full of praise, but what made it particularly gratifying was that I knew they wouldn't have been afraid to criticize if they'd felt it necessary. Friends like these are priceless.

A friend is someone you can confide in. With all the blabbermouths out there, it's nice to know there's someone you can talk to about private matters without worrying that your secrets will be divulged to others.

No one ever wants to ask herself, "Am I crazy or are those Cirque du Soleil ribbon dancers performing my decision to leave my husband and run off to Santa Fe with another woman?" A friend takes your vulnerability—and his responsibility—very seriously. When you call a friend and say, "Listen, there's something I have to get off my chest, but you have to promise not

A *real* friend would keep your secret.

to tell my parents, my girlfriend, any of my co-workers, the DEA, anyone who's visited Moscow in the past six months, the entirety of the leadership of the Church of Jesus Christ of Latter-day Saints, all non-unionized meatpackers, and Ralph Macchio," you know you can count on his discretion.

A friend is fun! Heck, most of the time, a friend is just someone you enjoy hanging out with, a compadre who shares your interests or your disdain for interests. When you're sitting home bored and want some company, what do you do? Well, sure, I guess you could try reanimating a corpse. But I bet you'd like a friend to help you, right? Or maybe you and your friend would rather play video games, bake double-chocolate-chip cookies from scratch, or watch the Zapruder film on a loop—whatever you enjoy doing, having a friend to share the experience with makes it that much more satisfying.

A friend will happily drown for you. Next time you're struggling in a rip current, pay careful attention to how your friends onshore react. Do they charge into the surf, not knowing or caring what the risks are? Or do they seem surprisingly torn between saving you and continuing to play with a Nerf ball? Either way, you're about to learn a lot about your friends.

Acquaintances: Middling the Waters

An acquaintance is someone with whom you have a slight relationship, one that's cordial but superficial—a co-worker, a fellow gym member, your father. You can think of an acquaintance as someone who doesn't know you well enough to give you an organ but might swing by your funeral. An acquaintance is something else, too: a friend just waiting to happen, albeit not necessarily to you. Some of us have all the friends we can handle—heck, some of us have Cinco de Mayo parties with their own zip codes—but most people could use another friend or two. What's the best way to elevate an acquaintanceship into something *real*?

1. *Break the context.* You typically interact with an acquaintance in a single environment. Maybe he's a neighbor you chat with in the mailroom, a member of your book club, or a fellow insomniac who haunts the same all-night laundromat you do. These encounters provide you with a regular setting for interaction, which means you don't have to rush things—there will almost certainly be another chance for you to explain exactly what you meant when you accused the government of using iPods to reprogram our dreams. But true friendship isn't bound to one coincidental location. It's deliberate and portable. And the longer you wait to upgrade your acquaintanceship, the more difficult it will be for you to break out of the situation to which you've grown so accustomed. So, pay attention to your acquaintance, learn about him, then use what you've learned to take the next step.

> SAL: Hi, Joel! You know, I've enjoyed throwing my life away at the dog track with you these past few weeks.

FAQ Buddy: Common Questions About Friends With Benefits

You might think it's strange and a little unkind of me to be bringing up this topic. After all, platonic friendships mystify you as it is, so what's the point in adding another inaccessible layer? It's a bit like trying to teach someone how to juggle four balls when they still haven't learned how not to chew on three. I don't have the time, space, or extensive clinical vocabulary required to address your intimate predilections, but I thought you should have at least some basic understanding of friendships that have a sexual component. (*Friends with benefits*, or *FWBs*, are also known as *fuck buddies, buddies with benies*, and *work-study students*.)

So, how does this work?

Everyone has sexual urges, even, sadly, old people. Sure, you can ease these feelings through self-stimulation or by sublimating them into a written work, but nothing can replace the release another person can offer. One-night stands can be awkward, however, and relationships too demanding. An FWB provides a certain level of companionship but without all the expectations. It's typically for people who pride themselves in their independence but who see some measure of safety in having a regular partner. It's like screwing someone on your bowling team.

Wow. Where do I get one?

Having existing friends would help. You could ask yourself

who among them seems emotionally positioned for this sort of arrangement and capable of being at least intermittently aroused by you. If you come up empty, you're out of luck. Unless, of course, you want to peruse the hundreds and hundreds of ads on Craigslist. I'll be writing more on Craigslist in the next chapter, but I'll just remind you now that there's at least a 30 percent chance that a particular ad was placed by some sort of Bigfoot.

Do I actually go out with my FWB?
It's up to you to set up comfortable boundaries, but of course you can go out. You might not want to make it too elaborate, and going dutch might be a good idea, but there's no reason you can't catch a movie, attend a poetry reading, or explore the mysteries of the deep at Epcot's Living Seas pavilion.

What concerns should I have?
You should watch for emotional escalation. You may be put in a position where you'll have to decide whether you want a greater commitment or none at all. You'll know your arrangement is heading in this direction when your FWB wants to discuss "getting closer," "firming up the relationship," or "sharing each other's blood somehow." On the other hand, an FWB who's bored of your company will sometimes try disengaging from all but the most carnal aspects of the relationship. You'll know your FWB is withdrawing from you when he says, "I'd like to get your clothes off using not only the fewest, but also the shortest, words possible."

Duly noted. Hey, have you had a friend with benefits?
Sure, lots. But they always cut it off almost immediately out of concern that our sexual relations are putting the friendship in jeopardy. They all say pretty much the same thing: "I never, ever want to do that again. You have the muscle tone of gravy, but your caress has all the tenderness of a nail gun. I'd rather eat you—literally cook and eat your flesh—than find myself again in your arms." And they have a point. It's not easy striking the balance between friendship and romance, and sometimes it's best to de-escalate before someone gets hurt.

JOEL: I've also enjoyed your company!

SAL: Maybe we could hang out somewhere else as well. I remember you expressing interest in professional hockey, getting even with your former boss, and hiring an escort, a high-class one with her own Web site and the titties God gave her, no balloons. Would you like to do something along those lines?

JOEL: Sounds terrific!

2. *Make a call.* You're not done yet. Yes, you signaled your interest in friendship and received an encouraging response, but you have to follow up. This not only reinforces your enthusiasm, but also provides the other person with an out. See, it's possible that your acquaintance actually wanted to decline your invitation but was too polite or spineless to do so. Maybe he's just too busy with

work or school for a new friend, or maybe he already has more friends than he can handle. Or maybe he's just, you know, all set with you. You'll start to get a sense of the person's real feelings toward you once you're no longer face to face.

MICHELLE:	Hi, Shruti! It's Michelle! I'm calling to confirm our brunch plans for Sunday. I'm really looking forward to it, and I hope you are, too. Are we still on?
SHRUTI:	Oh, I'm not feeling so well, unfortunately. How about another time?
MICHELLE:	Heck, it's only Tuesday now. Maybe you'll feel better by Sunday.
SHRUTI:	Nope.

Before you get too suspicious, remember that people sometimes have legitimate reasons for being unavailable—they *do* get sick, their rodeo-clown reserve units *do* get called up suddenly—and if that's the case, rescheduling should be easy. But if all they can offer are excuses, they're probably trying to drop a hint, and you shouldn't prolong their discomfort. If you're fairly convinced that the Walk for Hunger doesn't take place five times a week or that "chronic nose failure" is a made-up disease, just let the person go. Better to concentrate on the people you're making progress with, which brings us to step three.

3. *Express your gratitude.* A budding friendship is a tenuous connection, and people often worry about whether they're

holding up their end. Well, don't give them anything to worry about! Let your new friend know how much you appreciate the time you've spent together.

> DANA: You know, it's been really cool hanging out with you.

But don't make too big a deal about it—disproportionate gratitude will only come off as unseemly.

> DANA: You know, it's been really cool hanging out with you. I just want you to know how excited I am about our friendship. By the way, I'm getting risky limb-lengthening surgery so I can be as tall as you are.

How Many Friends Are Enough?

How would you like for me to reduce more than 150 years of evolutionary research into a couple of oversimplified half-truths? Done. In evolution, there are basically two strategies for passing on your genes: the male strategy, which involves impregnating as many females as possible in the hope that at least some meager fraction of the offspring will survive long enough to pass your genes on again, and the female approach, which calls for fewer mates but greater investment in the offspring. (You will notice that staying home to download nude depictions of Kim Possible is not considered a viable genetic strategy.) Friendship presents similar alternatives: Is it better to have lots of friends whom you don't spend much time with or a few close chums you see fairly often? The chart on page 150 will help.

Putting the "End" in "Friend"

Given the poverty of companionship in your life right now, you probably can't imagine cutting loose anyone who would be willing to be your friend. You'd go to outrageous lengths to explain away your friend's behavior—"Cigarette burns are just her way of saying thanks" or "It's perfectly legal in certain countries. In certain centuries"—because anything's better than solitude, right? Well, you couldn't be more somewhat mistaken. Yes, solitude is a drag, but sometimes, for all the companionship they provide, friends become burdensome. Maybe they're too needy, maybe they have much less in common with us than they used to, or maybe they make us look fat. Despite all the effort we put into a friendship, sometimes we have to move on. Unlike romantic relationships, which typically end with a breakup conversation, friendships often just languish and die without any mutual acknowledgment. This spares you the discomfort of a confrontation, but it might take some time for your friend to realize you've moved on. Here's how you help her along.

Mixed messages are key. It's human nature: People don't want to hear that their friendship no longer matters. They want to realize it for *themselves* after being strung along for a series of weeks or months. To set this in motion,

An Interview With a Pal

When I was younger, I had no friends, of course. The autograph sections of my yearbooks were filled with the names of sympathetic cafeteria workers and the forged signatures of my favorite ThunderCats. Sometimes, the cafeteria workers' names were forged as well. Of course, it's a very different story now. Everyone I meet wants to get to know me better or name a star after me or put me into an erotic pose. As you can imagine, it wasn't easy finding just the right friend to interview. My friends tend to be in-demand types who guard their image carefully. Finally, one person stood out from all the others.

CHARLES: Walnuts.

Sorry, I meant to get another Charles. Let's try again.

JASON: Tell the readers something of the history of our friendship.

CHARLES: Well, the *very* first time I saw you, you were exiting an adult bookstore.

JASON: Let me just interrupt for a second to tell the readers that "adult" books are pornographic books. Some of them might not be aware of this. I certainly wasn't when I entered that establishment.

CHARLES: Okay, well, you had this huge sack of stuff you weren't aware of.

JASON: Moving on. We actually first spoke in a cooking class, right?

CHARLES: Right. I took a cooking class at an adult-education center because I thought it might be a good way to meet women. Instead, it was just fifteen disillusioned men staring into their fondue. But you made eye contact, smiled, presented approachable body language, and gave me a firm handshake. Then you said, "Hello! I took this class because I'm the type of guy who can mess up a glass of ice water! Why did you decide to take this class, and what might you count among your other hobbies?" It all seemed a little canned and forced, but you seemed nice enough.

JASON: What has my friendship meant to you?

CHARLES: Well, over the years, any time I've needed someone to lean on—someone I can be, you know, real with—you've always been the one to get around to returning my calls eventually.

JASON: Oh, crud, that reminds me! I meant to tell you how much you have to live for a few weeks ago. I'm sorry, I've just been gardening so much as of late.

CHARLES: I've moved on.

JASON: My readers have trouble finding friends. If they're lucky, they have a few shallow acquaintances. Their pets even have an uncanny knack for breaking free and finding their way back to the pound. What advice would you have for these people?

CHARLES: Well, I'm not an expert, of course, but—

> | JASON: | Don't worry about it then. It was irresponsible of me to have asked. Think you're up for some rapid-fire word association? |
> | CHARLES: | Sure. Fire away. |
> | JASON: | "Friend." |
> | CHARLES: | "Loyal." |
> | JASON: | That was great, Charles. Thanks. |

begin to approach your friend with a maddening combination of enthusiasm and vagueness.

> | RICHARD: | That'd be great! We'll definitely have to do that at some point. |
> | MARTIN: | At some point? It's my New Year's Eve party. There's just that one point. |
> | RICHARD: | Awesome! Just give me a call whenever, and we'll see when we can make it happen. |

Communicate poorly. Please note that I'm not suggesting you ignore your friend entirely—how would you feel if your friend shut you off like a light switch? It's better to let your friend's e-mails sit in your inbox for weeks before replying. Do likewise with phone messages, and, when you finally do call back, make sure you're unable to talk very long. It's best to do this from a cell phone outside your home, so you can manufacture any number of plausible reasons for disconnecting: the subway's about to enter a tunnel, you have to deploy your parachute, and so on. Under perfect circumstances, much of your call will be cluttered with background noise—traffic or construction, for example. I myself often place these calls from monkey cages, but what's important is that there be some ambient distraction that strains the conversation. With any luck, the other person will pick up on the fact that you simply aren't giving him your undivided attention anymore. A former friend of mine used these techniques on *me*. It took me months, but I finally had to ask myself, "Why does she only call me when she's simultaneously about to jump into a meeting and in the middle of a Zeppelin laser light show?"

Change your look. When you finally consent to meet with your friend (avoiding him entirely would be hurtful), you can startle him with the new you. For example, if you're something of a preppy, you can show up in ripped jeans; if you're more of a hipster, you can show up in ripped jeans that were actually ripped by you and not by fabric-defacing robots, and you can further alarm your friend with comments such as "Why do we worship Bukowski like we do?" If you're an animal activist, drag an elk carcass into the coffee shop; if you're a writer, decline the fourteenth drink. Your goal is simply to behave in a way that your friend will find uncomfortably out of character. But don't mention the transformation. If your friend makes a remark, you can simply say, "I haven't changed. Maybe *you've* changed. Maybe you're only noticing my Jamaican accent now because it's become a problem for you. Who *are* you nowadays? And by the way, because I'm Jamaican, I meant to call you 'mon' a couple of times."

Deflect, deflect, deflect. That last example brings up an important point: Who's really to blame here? Okay, you, indisputably, but you still want to frame the situation as a matter that's open to interpretation. After all, there's nothing anyone appreciates more than an elaborate head game. Remember: You don't want to be the one to actually end the friendship; you just want to frustrate your friend to the point that, out of sheer exhaustion, *she* finally pulls the plug. Then, from your victimized perch, you can sniffle back tears and say, "Oh, I see. If that's how you want it, I won't stop you." If she ends it in person, you can stagger off in a daze, making sure to bump into at least one newspaper dispenser or mailbox.

Out of the Woodwork, Into the Fire

I have excellent news for you. If you've read this book carefully—but not carefully enough to uncover all the inconsistencies—you're now prepared to go out and get the friends you've been deprived of for so long and for so many defensible reasons. But how and where, exactly? When we observe a group of friends in our everyday lives, we sometimes forget that they were once total strangers, that they haven't been playing Frisbee golf together since the dawn of time. They had to meet *somewhere*, and they probably made some sort of effort to get to that somewhere. And now it's your turn. In the next chapter, I'll help you sort out some of the more common approaches to expanding your social circle, and, since your current social circle can fit inside the hole of a Froot Loop, there's no time to lose.

THE SITUATION	MANY CASUAL FRIENDS	A FEW CLOSE FRIENDS	NO FRIENDS
YOU NEED TO BORROW A HAMMER TO HANG A PICTURE	Lots of people willing to lend you one.	Have to wait till friends get home. Could be a while.	Picture looks pretty okay on top of the radiator, right?
IT'S SATURDAY NIGHT! WHAT'S YOUR PLAN?	So many people I can call. So few truly care if I do …	The usual crew. It's like some kind of chain gang, except we get Ethiopian food together.	My TV's broken, so I'm watching broken TV.
HOW'D YOUR PARTY GO?	Loads of people showed up, but none hung around very long. Like a BYOB subway platform.	The usual crew again. They stayed late and even helped with the cleanup. Am I horrible for being a little tired of them?	My seven-layer dip still has seven layers. Does that answer your cruel question?
THE FLU IS REALLY GETTING ANNOYING	"Get well soon, and remind us you exist as soon as you're feeling better."	"Here's some unsolicited chicken soup and magazines."	"Here's some unsolicited chi—sorry, wrong apartment. Go back to your fever dreams."
YOU JUST HATE EVERYTHING	"Bummer. Well if you change your mind about the improv show, one of us will have his cell on."	"Sit tight, I'll be there with a six pack in a few minutes."	"You poor thing! Paper or plastic?"

Oh, the Humanity!

Chapter 10

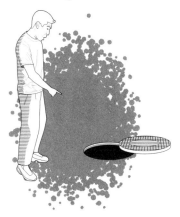

Where Will I Find My Friends?

They're out there. Deep down you know it. And yet, the more you howl "I need a friend!" out your window, the *less* interested people seem to be in getting to know you. But if you listen hard enough—beneath your neighbors' stereos, the police sirens, and, if you live in far northern climates, the walruses—you can probably hear someone saying, "Yeah, me too." How do you find this person? Well, it's a little like a treasure hunt with less digging and more salsa-dancing classes. And this chapter is your map.

Before we look at specific meeting places, I want to emphasize that putting yourself out there requires a willingness to undergo stressful states. Among social psychologists, this is known as the WUSS factor. Thanks to thousands of years of hardship, humans are predisposed to be wary of new environments. We never knew what sort of predators were lurking in the shadows, and, though you're unlikely to be devoured at a *Gilmore Girls* meetup, the precariousness of the situation can still make you anxious. And because you've explored so little, because you're intimidated by the cool spot on your pillow, there's a lot for you to be nervous about. Now, although I can assure you that the lessons in this book will see you through the most convoluted social situation, they won't do you any good unless you're willing to put them to work.

Are you ready? Let's see what's out there! Look, there's your door. Now open it!

You need to unlock it first.

No, the knob was locked, not the deadbolt. You actually just engaged the deadbolt, so now you'll have to go back and unlock it. All set? Good.

Try *pulling*.

Finding Your Fit

I once appeared on a game show called *Supermarket Sweep*, in which contestants dashed through a grocery store filling their carts with as much food as possible. The team whose purchases cost the most was the winner. My team lost because I kept stopping to read the ingredients. While that might have been in the best interest of my health, it was incompatible with the competition I had signed up for—no one was to blame, but the fit just wasn't there. As you venture out into the world, think about where *you* might fit best. People socialize in different places for different reasons, and I've listed a few of the more popular settings below.

1. Adult-education courses. Imagine a place that combined the structure of school with the rigor of skipping school. Sure, there are classes, but there are no grades, attendance is barely monitored, and the instructors teach simply because they love a subject, not because they know it. You might have thought about taking an adult-education course but were too intimidated by the catalog in the pizza place. Well, there's nothing to worry about. In fact, adult-education classes are a great way to meet people. For one thing, you have an interest in common with everyone else in the class right away, and that makes it easy to start a conversation. You can't just turn to a stranger at the bank and say, "How are your fruit sketches coming?" but you can feel perfectly comfortable doing that to someone in your Drawing for Beginners course. And from there, the conversation just takes off. Take Meg and Brooke, for example.

> **MEG:** I really like this German class. Are you studying it because you're traveling or just for fun?
>
> **BROOKE:** A little of both!
>
> **MEG:** Maybe we can practice a dialogue sometime. Pronunciation's tricky, and I'm wretchedly alone.

| BROOKE: | Sounds good! It's much easier to practice conversation with another person. Plus, if I disappeared tomorrow, few would notice and fewer would care. |
| MEG: | Great, I'll give you a call! *Auf Wiedersehen!* |

Adult-education courses have an intermediate duration, which means they'll end eventually but will last long enough for you to meet most of your classmates and find out which ones you feel most compatible with. If the class is large, you might want to assist your memory by jotting down some notes about each person.

Alfonso = too stuck up

Hannah = too pretty

Anne = too nice, probably wants something unspeakable

Morgan = too smart, will use equations to bully me somehow

Edward = too old

Larry = too almost old

Wayne = studded belt too menacing

Toshiko = too on the other side of the room

Wendy = whatever's on her medical ID bracelet could be a hassle down the road

Brady = suspiciously normal

Veronica = likes me, must be psychotic

2. *Volunteering.* Volunteering has one immediate and obvious advantage over adult-education classes: cost. Believe it or not, volunteer groups won't charge you a penny of tuition to pick up syringes along the beach. That's not as

much fun as many adult-education classes, but you do get the satisfaction of contributing to humanity at large, and the next time someone accuses you of being self-absorbed you'll have something to point to besides having watched part of Farm Aid. You won't be pitching in alone, of course, and your fellow volunteers will probably be generous, open-minded people. What does this mean for you? Well, anyone who would give up a Saturday to floss the homeless will very likely give you a chance as a friend. On the other hand, if you come off as too tragic, spending time with you will be converted into a volunteer cause in itself. You'll know this is occurring when everyone at your party is wearing a T-shirt with your name and the United Way logo on it.

3. *Pub crawls.* When you're alone, pubs can be intimidating. For one thing, most people aren't there by themselves, which means they aren't necessarily interested in meeting new people. And they might view the fact that you're by yourself with suspicion, no matter how often you expectantly glance at your watch or stage fake cell-phone conversations. But don't throw your hands up and say "I'm not good enough to watch ESPN on mute with these people" just yet. There's always a pub crawl.

When you sign up for a pub crawl, you unite with a group of strangers and tour a series of bars, downing a specified number of drinks at each. Sometimes the crawls target establishments that are easy stumbling distance from each other, while others go for a clever theme like

"It's Martini Time" or "Drinks That Taste Like Cake Frosting." You can make friends with the people in your group or with others you encounter along the way. It's all about meeting new folks—until the eleventh drink, at which point it's about screwing the person you threw up on least. But before you register for your crawl, ask around and make sure it's a good one. By way of example, I offer the itinerary for a crawl I once put together myself, an event so notorious that no one even *dared* to sign up for a second installment.

Dear Fellow Debauchers,

Saturday night's boozefest is locked and loaded! Except for being pushed back until late afternoon on Sunday. I forgot my mother and I had tickets to *Mamma Mia!* But, trust me, you lost souls had better rest up those overgrown beer steins you call bodies. If I may refer to these T-shirts I just had made: "White Makes Right!" What? No, no, they're supposed to say "The Walk for Liquor" on the front and "There Is No Cure" on the back. Will anyone feel uncomfortable turning their hate shirt inside out and writing in my funny lines with a marker? I can lend you a marker.

Anyway, here's an updated version of our inebriation itinerary. Just some minor alterations:

5:00 P.M. I just learned that TOM O'SKELLY'S ALEHOUSE AND GRILLE became a Pier 1 Imports fairly recently. So, I'm thinking we meet up at the papasan chairs, where I'll do a quickie head count. You might want to buy a nice window treatment while you're there—after all, this will be your last respectable day on Earth!

6:00 P.M. Originally, I had penciled in FATTY'S LOUNGE as our little dive adventure. But when I called to ask whether they could accommodate our posse of drunken professionals, the guy on the phone just said, "No survivors," and hung up. That's OK, because we can use this slot to grub up for the journey into the abyss that lies ahead.

This might be a good time to mention the disco bus. As it turns out, the company doesn't run it on Sundays. But I've got my Hyundai Accent. And my sister says she'll try to lend me the strobe light her daughter had left over from last year's Drama Club haunted house. I'm not sure if that's the kind of thing I can plug into the cigarette lighter, though.

We have a pro-vs.-con situation. On one hand, the Accent, unlike the bus, is equipped with side-impact airbags. But on the other hand, since I can't fit more than five people in my car, the rest of you maniacs will have to cruise with my grandfather. He's agreed to drive provided that you comport yourselves like ladies and gentlemen, and that you not go on and on about his snoring. He also has several meteorological phobias, one of which is good weather, the ominous atmospheric state that always immediately precedes bad weather.

7:30 P.M. The madness begins. Soon. First, the Corona Convoy has to stop at the CHINESE-AMERICAN VOCATIONAL ADVANCE-MENT CENTER, because I have to tutor. I usually work with refugees on Wednesday nights, but I canceled the last two weeks and promised "Reggie" we'd get together over the weekend. He's got a big interview coming up, and we need to catch up on occupational vocabulary. Legally, I can't leave you outside unattended, so I was thinking the bacchanal could move indoors and quietly look at flash cards or something.

9:00 P.M. Y'all want this party started, right? Please keep your hands inside the vehicle at all times, because this coaster-of-the-damned is rollin' on! However, I'm going to have to first head home and GIVE MY PARAKEET HIS EAR MEDICATION. The good news is that this usually doesn't take more than fifteen minutes or so. The bad news is that I don't like to wake him if he's asleep, so I'm eliminating the 10:00 P.M. and 11:00 P.M. stops just in case we have to wait it out a little while.

12:00 A.M. Time to slap your inhibitions on the ass and send 'em on home. After I drop off some videos, we're off to hot spot THE MANATEE ROOM. Now, *normally* you have to know someone to get into the Manatee Room. So, we probably won't get in. But if I'm not mistaken, there's an adult movie theater down the block, and you'd think the people there would be able to direct us to a package store in the area. If that doesn't work, I might ask one of the ladies to FELLATE A HOBO in exchange for his flask.

That's it. Those are the only changes. Also, two reminders: In the event anything happens on the pub crawl, it *stays* on the pub crawl. And you'll have to return those T-shirts to me before you head home. They're actually rentals.

Glug, glug,
Jason

4. Cults. Hear me out. First of all, cults don't start out as bad ideas. A group of people find themselves disenchanted with the values or gun laws of contemporary society and separate themselves to create something better. All is well until one day the leader says something like "You know, I think I want all the women." While it's true that joining a cult entails forfeiting most of your worldly possessions and all existing personal ties, you should at least consider the social benefits. For one thing, you'll never again have to worry about making friends. They will be assigned to you and will probably die nearby. In fact, everything I've talked about in this book so far will cease to be a concern. Forget chapter two. You'll never have to impress anyone with a joke.

RYAN-GA: Why is Paris Hilton like a pet store?

SONIA-GA: That, like all mysteries, will be revealed when our souls are welcomed into their new vessels on Omnocron Delta G.

RYAN-GA: Oh, you've heard that one before!

Tech Support

It seems that now, more than ever, the best way to meet people is to stay home not meeting them. No matter what you're into, there's a place for you on the Web. Pick any interest, drop a few *w*'s in front of it, and you've found yourself a community. But before we talk about what the computer has to offer, I want to pay tribute to a meeting place whose popularity is dwindling fast: the party line.

The party line. Back when people watched *Perfect Strangers* with a straight face and famine in Ethiopia was totally barfing us out, the best technology available for making friends was your phone, possibly the football phone you received free with your subscription to *Sports Illustrated*. That's all changed. Although most people have turned to the Internet, you can still catch the ads for chat lines on late-night television: Sometimes they'll feature two sexy women who decided to stay in for the evening and wear negligees; or a stylish, gorgeous man calling from behind the wheel of his sports car; or a muscular construction worker just kind of standing there in cutoffs. Whoever's in the ad sure seems glad they dialed the line. And why wouldn't they be? It's true that people occasionally abuse these services by instigating raunchy conversations, but, like you, lots of people are just calling to hang out.

CALLER ONE:	Hello?
CALLER TWO:	Hello?
CALLER THREE:	Any chicks out here?
CALLER FOUR:	Hello?
CALLER TWO:	I think it's just dudes.
CALLER FIVE:	Hello?
YOU:	Hi! I haven't called before! Any tips for a newbie? I enjoy indie films and contemporary art. How do you like to spend your free time?
CALLER SIX:	Hello?

CALLER TWO:	Where the ladies at?
CALLER SEVEN:	Hello?

Craigslist. I hesitate to comment on a specific Web site because you never know when it will shut down or just cease to be culturally relevant. (Of course, if cultural relevance were really a concern, I wouldn't have written a *book* to begin with.) But the online bulletin board Craigslist is kind of a phenomenon and probably has the staying power to last at least until this book is remaindered or pulped and fed to cattle. On Craigslist, at no cost to yourself, you can place ads or respond to ads from people just like you. Look at the samples below.

> I'm looking for someone to play chess with. I've absorbed some basic strategies, but I still have a lot to learn. If you'd like to "check" me out, just write back and tell me about your chess background. Thanks.

> I want to start a book club in the Boston area. Kind of like Oprah, but maybe some less conventional stuff. Thanks!

> Calling all wannabe Monets! Do you enjoy painting outdoors? I do! It inspires me in a way that a studio can't. Anyway, if you'd like to break out the easel with me sometime, send at least one clear picture of your uncut cock. Thanks!

Hold on a sec. That last ad seems a little peculiar, doesn't it? Unfortunately, not everyone on the board is just looking for a friend. Sometimes it's obvious, and sometimes it's not. Consider the mixed messages in these ads.

I'm looking for a woman to check out the folk scene with. I'm a straight SWM, and I'm *not* interested in dating. I'm in pretty good shape, been told I look like an athletic Beck. But this is not a dating ad. I'm just looking for petite single women to chill with. Asian a big plus!

I like massages, so do you? I like the sensual touch together. This is NOT SEX! I just massage you and then you can return the massage to me. I am trained massage professional, so my hands are educated and clever! No man, gay or not, just pretty young woman. I can bring wetness oils to your place, okay? NOT SEX!!! I will say no to anyone who says hello to sex!

If you have to think too hard about the intentions of an ad, it's better to move on, especially since you can place one of your own. As you sift through your replies, focus on the people who took the time to introduce themselves. Pretend the chess ad I presented above was the one you placed on Craigslist. Would you really want to reply to someone who responded anonymously with "I'm down with checkers. Hit me back, bitch"?

~~Frien~~ *MySpace*. I'm well aware of the media saturation that MySpace has achieved. In fact, I fear the exposure has deprived me of the opportunity to make a quality sexual-predator joke, and that hurts a lot. If for some reason you've never explored MySpace, here's what you do. Show up and create a profile. (Your gender matters primarily in terms of the number of people who will immediately contact you promoting webcams.) Over time, friends—of a sort—will be drawn to you the same way algae collects around a buoy, and then you can enjoy each other's blogs, music, and zodiac signs. But be warned: logging off can be painful, because you're abruptly transitioning from the company of three thousand MySpace friends to the company of just a few real-life moths. Generally, there are two ways of dealing with this situation: Try to strike a healthy balance between your online and offline friendships so you won't feel totally disconnected even when signed out, or invite more moths into your home. Choose the approach that works best for you.

The New, Entirely Adequate You

In Kafka's short story "The Metamorphosis," Gregor Samsa wakes up one day mysteriously transformed into a human-sized insect. He eventually adjusts and is elected mayor. Like Samsa, you've undergone a punishing transformation but now find yourself standing at the edge of a world without boundaries, except, I guess, for that edge you're standing at. But you don't need me to tell you that, do you? You want to jump up and punch the wall, no longer because it's what you do to feel something, anything, but because nothing's going to stand in your way anymore.

But there is one more chapter. It's very short, but very, very important.

Chapter 11

Will You Be My Friend?

I'm torn. On one hand, declining your friendship would be like a master chef shunning her own soufflé or a bomb maker not blowing himself up. On the other hand, accepting it would be kind of weird, don't you think? Would your veneration be a distraction? Would we be able to enjoy a movie together, let alone a week at Epcot?

But what the heck. I'll give you a shot. After all, depending on how many copies of this book are sold, you either helped me retire or buy eight minutes of parking. I owe you something either way.

Okay, let's see … The guy who was hosting the party I was supposed to attend tonight got sick at the last second, so, remarkably, I don't have any plans. Tomorrow, I'm tentatively scheduled to check out a band with another friend, but there's a good chance he won't be able to get a babysitter, so I'll probably be free. There's a barbecue the following day, but it's supposed to rain, and if it doesn't, my friends said they'll all have jury duty simultaneously.

So, you know, I'll be around, pretty much.

A Moment of Self-Defense

If you're wondering whether I have the formal credentials to write this book, you should know that I earned a bachelor's degree in psychology. Very few institutions offer diplomas in this discipline, and only the most brilliant and dedicated undergraduates can survive the full four-year course of study. However, if you've discovered any inaccuracies, redundancies, or offenses to logic, I am sorry and will forward your criticisms to the copyeditor, who put them into the book as I slept unaware. If you're still not satisfied, I'll remind you that you found this book two shelves down from a compilation of *Garfield* comics.

Infinite Gratitude

John Warner not only oversaw this project but has published my work on McSweeney's Internet Tendency for several years now—thanks are long overdue. Jane Friedman at F+W Publications essentially made this book happen. Without her advocacy, none of these pages exist. Copyeditor Ed Page was nice enough to elevate my writing a grade level or two, and my agent, Michelle Brower, put my proposal in front of these people to begin with. Good thinking, there.

Credits

"Quiz: Are You Curious?" was adapted from a piece first appearing in *Yankee Pot Roast*, August 2006.

"But Enough About Me. Let's Talk About Yoplait: An Alternative to Idle Conversation" was adapted from "Talk Different: An Alternative to Idle Conversation," which appeared in *McSweeney's Internet Tendency*, August 2003.

"Amendments to the Pub Crawl" first appeared in *McSweeney's Internet Tendency*, September 2004.

About the Author

Jason Roeder's humor writing has been published in *The New Yorker, McSweeney's Internet Tendency,* and *Salon,* as well as the books *Created in Darkness by Troubled Americans: The Best of McSweeney's Humor Category* and *The Future Dictionary of America.* He lives in New York.

TOW BOOKS

THE TOW BOOKS STORY

BY JOHN WARNER, CHIEF CREATIVE CZAR

On August 18, 1948, my great uncle, Allan T. Warner (Tow Truck King of Tecumseh, Michigan), told a joke to Stanley Johnson as they bumped their way back to the repair shop following Stanley's latest driving mishap. To ease Stanley's upset, Uncle Allan turned to him and said, "Stanley, have you ever heard the one about the horse, the rabbi and the one legged duck who went into a bar ...?"

From that day forward, people who needed a tow from Warner Wrecking and Towing were treated to short entertainments, jokes, and yarns, spun by Uncle Allan himself.

To keep people from deliberately crashing their cars just to hear the latest offerings from Uncle Allan, he began collecting them in pamphlets and selling them out of his service station, giving birth to "The Official Warner Books" (TOW Books).

Over the next 25 years, TOW Books published 107 volumes. On August 26, 1973, Uncle Allan hung up his winch and released his final title, *A Rabbi, a One-Legged Duck and a Bunch of Dirty Hippies in a Volkswagen Bus With a Busted Distributor Who Don't Have Any Money, But Think It's Okay to Pay Hard Working People in "Good Karma" Walk Into a Bar and Get Their Teeth Kicked In Because They Deserve It.*

We're pleased to renew Uncle Allan's commitment to publishing "funny books for people with good senses of humor."